More Praise for Working Across Generations

"Paralyzed by reports and data, the field continues to be perplexed by the so-called generational crisis and how it should respond. Kunreuther, Kim, and Rodriguez offer a sober critique of work thus far, reframing the discussion as an opportunity, and move the reader to practical approaches that will likely transform the field."

—Patrick Corvington, senior associate,
The Annie E. Casey Foundation

"Headlines, research, and polls tell us that Gen Xers and millennials are influencing politics and the work of policy reform across the country. Now, thanks to authors Kunreuther, Kim, and Rodriguez, we see how they're working for positive change in their communities—often under the radar screen. By providing a comprehensive examination of this work, the authors show how transformation can be sustainable when different generations realize they can learn from each other and work together to create lasting change."

—Tamara Draut, director, Economic Opportunity
Program at Demos and author, *Strapped: Why America's
20- and 30-Somethings Can't Get Ahead*

"Finally! A breakdown of some of the most pressing leadership challenges we face today. *Working Across Generations* serves as a primer for nonprofits needing to transform structure, culture, and practices so that we are not only more effective, but also able to involve and sustain more people in this sector."

—Jane Sung E Bai, political education coordinator,
Social Justice Leadership

"If you are a long-term leader of a nonprofit organization or a newcomer to the field, you must read this book because it has useful insights and practical information about how to deal with leadership transition issues in both your own organization and the nonprofit sector as a whole."
—Frank J. Omowale Satterwhite, founder and senior advisor, National
Community Development Institute

"The generational shift in nonprofit leadership is full of drama, confusion, and exciting possibilities. *Working Across Generations* maps the trends and guides us toward solutions."
—Linda Burnham, cofounder and former executive director, Women of
Color Resource Center

Select tables and exercises identified with a Web icon in
the book *Working Across Generations: Defining the Future of
Nonprofit Leadership* are available free online. If you would like
to download and print out a copy of these materials, please visit:

www.josseybass.com/go/FrancesKunreuther

Working Across Generations

Defining the Future of Nonprofit Leadership

Frances Kunreuther

Helen Kim

Robby Rodriguez

JOSSEY-BASS
A Wiley Imprint
www.josseybass.com

Published by Jossey-Bass
A Wiley Imprint
989 Market Street, San Francisco, CA 94103-1741   www.josseybass.com

Library of Congress Cataloging-in-Publication Data

Kunreuther, Frances.
    Working across generations : defining the future of nonprofit leadership /
Frances Kunreuther, Helen Kim, Robby Rodriguez.
        p. cm.
Includes bibliographical references and index.
    ISBN 978-0-470-19548-2 (cloth)
        1. Nonprofit organizations—Management.   I. Kim, Helen.   II. Rodriguez, Robby,
1975-   III. Title.
HD62.6.K86 2008
658.4'092—dc22
                                                                    2008020973

Printed in the United States of America
FIRST EDITION
HB Printing   10 9 8 7 6 5 4 3 2 1

THE CHARDON PRESS SERIES

Fundamental social change happens when people come together to organize, advocate, and create solutions to injustice. Chardon Press recognizes that communities working for social justice need tools to create and sustain healthy organizations. In an effort to support these organizations, Chardon Press produces materials on fundraising, community organizing, and organizational development. These resources are specifically designed to meet the needs of grassroots nonprofits—organizations that face the unique challenge of promoting change with limited staff, funding, and other resources. We at Chardon Press have adopted traditional techniques to the circumstances of grassroots nonprofits. Chardon Press and Jossey-Bass hope these works help people committed to social justice to build mission-driven organizations that are strong, financially secure, and effective.

Kim Klein, Series Editor

Contents

Foreword

We need more leadership in this country and around the rest of the world, and while we have shelves full of books on leadership from the business press, there are few from the nonprofit world. There are even fewer by authors who are grounded in the conviction that no enduring change can take place from the top down.

It is at the community and grassroots level where those most affected by social policies take the lead in forging the kind of world they want for themselves and their children; this is where the action is. Since we may elect a community organizer—and a post–baby boomer, to boot—as the next president of the United States, this is a good time for *Working Across Generations* to appear and for it to be widely read.

Frances Kunreuther, Helen Kim, and Robby Rodriguez take a topic about which many platitudes are offered—the looming leadership crisis in the nonprofit world—and give a fresh perspective on it, with creative thinking too rarely seen on this subject. They understand the complexities and force us to think outside the boxes on organizational charts.

They understand that it is not possible to deal with leadership in a vacuum without considering the changing nature of the workplace—indeed, the way work is structured. Corporations, operating as they do in more rigorous markets than most nonprofits, realized this a long time ago, which is why many businesses have family-sensitive work policies and innovative staffing and management arrangements, while ostensibly values-driven nonprofits, even (and sometimes especially) social justice ones, carry on with rigidly hierarchical organizational charts and stinting policies on work-family balance issues.

Kunreuther, Kim, and Rodriguez understand all the points along the leadership pipeline: not only how to attract, support, and listen to emerging young leaders, many of them women and people of color who have too long been missing from leadership positions in the nonprofit world, and whose full contributions can change the workplace and the rest of the world, but also the legitimate needs of the generation that holds leadership now. Many cling to leadership positions not because they are selfish or desperate to maintain power, but because they cannot imagine an alternative future. They still have much to contribute but few ways to do so. Our individualistic society treats that as a personal issue, but in fact it is a societal and structural one, and we have to come up with solutions that work.

Finally, the authors understand that the reluctance of many younger nonprofit staffers to assume executive director positions—to take their place in the pipeline when opportunities emerge—has much to do with all the demands of fundraising, staff management, board maintenance, and external relationships. These are real issues, and often structural ones, and they too deserve our best collective thinking. The challenges that social justice organizations face—the widening income gap, the persistence of discrimination, the shredding of the social safety net, the crisis in education for poor children of color—demand the strongest leadership we can find. If we have to remake the workplace, and the way we think about what leadership is and how to find and support it, to do so, then there is no more urgent task before us. We are fortunate that Frances Kunreuther, Helen Kim, and Robby Rodriguez have turned their formidable minds and experiences to this subject, and I hope it sparks much discussion and action in the ranks of those in the nonprofit sector and on those who rely on its continued edge and effectiveness.

New York, New York   Gara LaMarche
May 2008   President
                            Atlantic Philanthropies

Acknowledgments

We start with our deep gratitude for all the individuals and organizations whose stories shaped the foundation of this book. Their candor and generosity, as well as their vision and commitment to social sector work, have motivated and challenged us to do our best to make a useful contribution to this field. We especially thank Susana Almanza, Gordon Chin, Andrew Friedman, Ellen Gurzinsky, Ng'ethe Maina, Jerome Scott, and Young Shin, whose reflections are highlighted in this book.

Board, staff, and members of the SouthWest Organizing Project deserve a special tribute. Their honesty, wisdom, humanity, and sometimes sheer will to move forward together during an often confusing and turbulent leadership and generational change process have been truly inspiring. We hope you agree as you get to know them in the following pages.

We acknowledge the work and support of many colleagues who made our work possible. Our original generational change study was done while Frances was at the Hauser Center for Nonprofit Organizations at Harvard University in 2001 with the help and support of her colleagues, especially Carol Chetkovich. At that time, not many paid attention to the issues around generational change in leadership. Since then, the increasing numbers of colleagues and resources have built a substantial body of work.

We cannot possibly name everyone whose work has influenced ours, but we thank a few people in particular. Ludovic Blain had the foresight to take our original study around the country to collect responses from Generation X leaders. We appreciate the continued support from the Annie E. Casey Foundation, especially Donna Stark, who gave the initial funds to explore the issue of generational leadership shift, and Patrick Corvington, whose contribution of ideas is reflected throughout this work. We also thank Linda Wood and the Haas Jr. Fund for their support and for Linda's thoughtful observations about building leadership.

Nancy Adess's adept editing was instrumental in bringing clarity to our manuscript, and Sujin Lee and Dahnesh Medora's patient review of the exercises in this book was indispensable. Heartfelt thanks to everyone at Jossey-Bass/Wiley for all their support in every phase of this book. The initial enthusiasm of Allison Brunner and Jesse Wiley gave us the push we needed, and the steady guidance of Allison's talented and patient team was truly a gift to us.

In addition to the three of us, the rest of the Building Movement Project team—Caroline McAndrews, Linda Campbell, Kim Klein, Emery Wright, Cory Isaacson, newest member Trish Tchume, and intern Payal Kapadia—provided an invaluable critique and support throughout the conception and writing of this book. We could not have asked for a more brilliant, supportive, and fun team behind us. Special kudos go to Caroline, who not only gave us detailed comments on our early book draft but also took on significant amounts of extra work with great competency and humor as this book was birthed.

We especially thank our colleague, series editor, coach, cheerleader, and friend Kim Klein. Without her steady guidance and unwavering belief in us, you would not be reading this book.

Finally, Frances acknowledges Ann Holder with love and gratitude for her personal and intellectual sustenance throughout this process. Robby thanks Jeanne Gauna, Michael Leon Guerrero, Joaquin Lujan, Eleanor Chavez, and Roberto Contreras for their support, commitment to social change, and the opportunity they have provided him. And Helen thanks her parents, John Changduk and Ellen Hyesook, from the bottom of her heart.

Introduction

It was 1980, and a bunch of twenty- and thirtysomethings started an organization with a vision of "empowering the disenfranchised of the Southwest to realize racial and gender equality and social and economic justice." They were revolutionaries—idealistic young activists who had come out of the civil rights, antiwar, women's, and power identity movements. With Ronald Reagan ushering in a tide of conservatism, they wanted to build strong organizations to maintain and move forward the gains of the 1960s and 1970s. They were serious about creating a new society. Fast-forward twenty-five years. It's 2005, and there I was, the newly appointed executive director of the SouthWest Organizing Project (SWOP). I am twenty-eight years old and mentored by some of those same visionaries. I have a deep respect and admiration for their work and feel a responsibility to carry forward their hopes and dreams.

(Deep breath. Inhale. Exhale.)

I took over the organization during a time of great transition. The founding director of the organization, Jeanne Gauna, had passed away after battling breast cancer. My codirector, Michael Leon Guerrero, had left SWOP to be near his family in California after seventeen years in the organization. I was mourning the loss of one mentor and wanting to support the decision of another.

Jeanne and Michael trusted me to carry on their legacy; I wasn't so sure.

SWOP had important work to do, but its ability to succeed was weighted by uncertainty. It was a living memorial to Jeanne, and I knew that Michael would not be able to move on with his life if he thought the organization was struggling. Allies wondered out loud, "What will happen now?" Funders were waiting to see what would become of SWOP without Jeanne or Michael. The pressure not to fail was enormous.

Half the staff was under thirty years old, and the entire board was fifty or older. We struggled with the change. The board, staff, and I were all extending ourselves in new ways by playing different roles in this new era. Still, there were disagreements, suspicions, and fear. Board members felt a heightened sense of responsibility to their oversight duties. I was learning that I couldn't assume the same level of authority that Jeanne and Michael had within the organization. Staff members were getting used to a different leadership style, added responsibilities, and shifts in organizational culture. Board, staff, and long-time members had different motivations for coming to this work, and depending on their generation, different personal experiences as well. But through new and shared experiences, we learned to trust each other and pulled through in a testament of our love for the organization and its work.—Robby, Generation Xer

The story of leadership change is being told across the United States. In business and the nonprofit social sector, in government and foundations, longtime leaders are talking about what they will do next and wondering who will take their place while new generations prepare for the future. It is a time of great hope and possibility, and a time of challenge and loss. Like Robby, younger leaders are coming forward to head organizations as older leaders begin to step aside or fall away.

This book is about changes in leadership: the shifts from one generation to the next in social sector organizations. (In this book we use *nonprofit sector* and *social sector* interchangeably.) We are at an especially important moment in the U.S. nonprofit sector. The generations that have been at the forefront of developing and leading organizations are thinking about the next phase of life. Baby boomers are hitting their sixties, and their predecessors, often referred to as the traditional generation, whom we call veterans for change here, are rapidly exiting the workforce. Generation Xers and the millennials are poised to step into new roles, looking for opportunities and evaluating whether they will be the next group of nonprofit and social sector leaders.

The upcoming generational shifts in leadership create a natural opportunity to take stock. We are moving from the baby-boom bulge and political touchstone of the 1960s movements to the globalized, connected, and yet polarized world that characterizes the first decade of the new millennium. Leadership change generates anxiety as well as high expectations. As we contemplate how to address issues ranging from the earth's sustainability to how to build a society without constant threats of violence, we look to leaders who can make a difference now.

This book offers those working in and affiliated with nonprofit groups the opportunity to prepare for how to proceed thoughtfully during this period. We offer information about how to approach leadership shifts and concepts in order to understand different generations of leaders in social sector organizations. We look at the impact of generational leadership transitions on individuals and point out what broader or more systemic issues need to be addressed. Finally, we recognize the need for leaders to be able to understand each other across real and sometimes frustrating generational divides. The book provides ideas and concrete tools for increasing communication and compassion so we can build bridges across what can sometimes seem like generational chasms.

We view leadership shifts as an opportunity, particularly if we pay attention to issues related to how a change in generations at the helm of nonprofits will affect organizations. Younger leaders will be different from older ones. To understand and give context to these differences, this book:

- Explores common assumptions about the upcoming transition between generations in the social sector.
- Introduces new ideas or frames for thinking about generational leadership change.
- Examines how this change poses individual, organizational, and systemic challenges for those in the social sector.
- Gives examples and provides exercises for how to address these issues.

The Nonprofit Sector and Social Change

The nonprofit sector is distinguished by its mission-driven work and values for the common good. Our primary focus in this book is on nonprofits that we call *social change organizations*.[1] These organizations are distinguished by their commitment to creating a just and sustainable world. They provide services, work with communities, promote the arts, advocate for policies, and fight legal battles with a view toward reducing injustice. Many grew out of efforts in the 1960s and 1970s to address inequality in the United States and in global society.

It is our experience that the issues facing social change groups are no different from those facing the nonprofit sector at large, especially in small and midsized organizations. Addressing leadership change is a common imperative across the sector, but smaller groups face particular difficulties. Time to think about leadership competes with the press of immediate work and the continual need to raise funds. In addition, long hours and low pay have been a hallmark of small and midsized organizations, and many have relied on leaders willing to dedicate their lives to the work. New leadership may not offer themselves as the same personal safety net for these groups. The transition will hit hard, and nonprofits that do not prepare for leadership and generation change may find that their very survival is at risk.

What Is a Generation?

For decades sociologists have attempted to understand what forms a generation and the meaning generations have in society. Karl Mannheim's essay, "The Problem of Generations," explains that a generation is the same age cohort that lives through the same significant events, especially during adolescence or young adulthood.[2] In other words, a generation is shaped not only by the era but also by pivotal events, such as World War II or the civil rights movement or the attacks on the World Trade Center. These events symbolize shared reference points and common experiences. For example, those in the "greatest generation" came of age during World War II, which influenced their shared understanding of heroism, the need to save the world from evil, the meaning of sacrifice, and the importance of loyalty. Those born in other eras can listen to their stories but will not have the same visceral sense when a song comes on the radio or a name is mentioned as those in that generation.

A generation has a shared memory of important events and similar assumptions about what matters based on their formative experiences. Naturally there are subgroups by areas such as region, class status, and race/ethnicity, but there are also common markers. Not everyone in a generation has shared experiences; moreover, some experiences are more universal and others are more particular.

In this book we talk about four generations: veterans of change, baby boomers, Generation X and millennials. We are aware that the way we refer to the characteristics of each generation is a simplification. Dates that delineate the generations are disputed, and there are many different experiences, beliefs, and actions within each of these generational cohorts. But defining generations in broad strokes helps us to navigate the large shifts that will be taking place over the next decades in nonprofit and social change leadership. Not only will the people in these positions change, but there will also be changes in the way the leadership is enacted. That is the essence of generational differences.

Four generations are currently in the workplace:

- Veterans of change (born 1925–1945), often referred to as the traditional or silent generation. In social change work, this generation pioneered the formation of new organizations. They are noted for their top-down style of management, sense of propriety and loyalty, and emphasis on commitment, especially to their organizations.
- Baby boomers (born 1946–1964), the post–World War II generation whose younger members are sometimes called *Cuspers*. Almost 80 million people, they assume they have the power to make change; they believe in hierarchy but also try to be more inclusive in the workplace.
- Generation X (born 1965–1979), a cohort of 45 million, also referred to as the sandwich generation because of their position between two larger generations. They are more skeptical than the boomers and more self-reliant. Xers enjoy working with their peers, chafe at being told what to do, and stress results.
- Millennials (born 1980–2000), also known as Generation Y and the Echo Generation, rival the boomers in size. Self-confident millennials now in the workforce believe they will make a difference through their practical know-how.

Popular literature explaining the generations abounds. Books such as *The Greatest Generation, Boomer Nation, 13th Gen*, and *Millennials Rising* define the characteristics and shared experiences of these generations.[3] Another set of books is focused on the workforce, with titles such as *Generations at Work, Managing Generation X, Leadership Divided, Retiring the Generation Gap, Bridging the Generation Gap*, and *When Generations Collide*.[4] Generational change is a media and marketing phenomenon. Newspapers have separate sections geared to retiring baby boomers, magazine covers show the new leaders in Generation X and now millennials, and the Internet offers connections among different generational cohorts.[5] Generational differences are referred to by presidential candidates, venture capitalists, movement builders, and media mavens. The nonprofit literature on generation change was slower to develop but is now in full swing. Monographs and articles address executive transitions, generations of leadership, and changing giving patterns based on age.[6] Studies focus on when executives plan to leave their jobs, and why.[7] New reports have been released on the attitudes and plans of the younger generations in the workforce.[8] And there is research on what will happen to older leaders, statistical models of how many vacant positions will need to be filled in the coming decades, and studies of differences among generations of leaders.[9] Peter Brinckerhoff, in *Generations: The Challenge for a Lifetime in Your Nonprofit*, describes how generational change will affect the nonprofit sector at large.[10] There has also been analysis of the nonprofit workforce, especially the work of Paul Light, who has examined whether there will be new generations of nonprofit and public sector workers.[11] In addition, almost every large nonprofit gathering has a workshop, presentation, or material about executive transitions.

What Is Different in This Transition?

We are frequently asked why we focus on generation change in nonprofits. After all, moving from one generation to the next is nothing new; it's been done for centuries. Why is this transition in leadership different from any other? As the book unfolds, we emphasize that there are particular characteristics based on the circumstances and experiences that define the generations. These, along with the evolution of nonprofit organizations over the past forty years, will set the stage for the tasks of new leadership.

Nonprofits Evolving

The veterans of change and baby boom activists were part of the wave of growth in nonprofits during the 1960s and 1970s. As part of the movement activities of the time, they pressed the federal government to take more responsibility for alleviating poverty and building communities by supporting organizations to provide livable housing, primary health care, decent jobs, and cultural pride. New funding, public and private, gave birth to organizations designed to make life better for poor and other marginalized communities. There were programs for battered women, low-income youth and children in foster care, people with addictions, the homeless and hungry, preschoolers and the elderly, and many other groups. Leaders, staff, and board members had high hopes that things would get better, especially for people without the resources or status to have their voices heard.[12]

Starting the Retrenchment

Just as these groups were hitting their stride, things started to change. In 1980, the election of Ronald Reagan signaled a conservative backlash. As tax cuts reduced the federal funds available to nonprofits, many groups reframed their work or expanded into new areas and pressed local government to pick up the slack in order to continue to serve their communities. Organizations that did not receive public funds sought out foundations and individual donors for resources to fight the policies that left many people more vulnerable.

Over time publicly funded nonprofits found they were spending less time holding government accountable and more time trying to provide vital services. Advocacy organizations and organizing groups were forced into a defensive position to keep what existed rather than to push for more. Meanwhile, conservatives raised questions about nonprofits and their impact. They attacked the sector, as they did government, as rife with bloated bureaucratic structures, accusing them of counting contracts rather than making change.

In the 1990s, nonprofit leaders had some impressive successes in obtaining public funds to address the needs of their communities, such as in HIV and AIDS. Still, it took constant vigilance and flexibility to obtain the money to keep programs running. The theme of individual responsibility was echoed in the shift from government grants to reimbursement fees for groups providing community-based services. Some organizations grew by taking on more responsibilities as government devolved its work in such areas as child welfare and health services. Others, such as legal services for the poor, had to scramble when large portions of public funds were eliminated. Organizations felt the pressure from private foundations too, which urged them to diversify their funding sources. Many organizations began to look for more private dollars from individuals or turn to earned income.

The Business of Outcomes

As the year 2000 approached, the business model took hold in many nonprofits. The idea of empowerment—once about finding ways to support economic and political power in low-income and marginalized communities—took on new meaning with clients rebranded as "consumers" who could make choices about the services they received and were held accountable for deciding whether (or not) to make changes in their own lives.

There was also the measurable outcomes revolution. It was no longer good enough to count the people who came through the organization's doors or to show positive marks on "consumer" surveys. Now groups had to demonstrate their impact. Proving effectiveness appealed to funders, who wanted a sense of how their investments had made a difference. They began to seek more rigorous evaluation of the organizations they supported. Groups were asked for their logic model or theory of change, that is, to make explicit their reasoning for why their programs were or could be successful.

These techniques helped organizations grapple with whether they were really accomplishing their goals and pushed them to think about their results. But as funders sought evidence for the claims organizations made about their accomplishments, a systemic analysis of problems and their long-term solutions was forced to take a back seat in order to prove short-term results. Outcome measures helped groups focus on what they had accomplished but also constrained them as they tried to meet the reporting requirements of different funding sources.

Demands for outcomes and the reduction of government funds led to new strategies for nonprofit sustainability. Following the spirit of the entrepreneurial revolution, groups considered how to find new income streams, developed business plans, talked about going to scale, and lobbied for earmarks from local and federal government. Some started endowments and capital campaigns. Others looked to venture capitalists for investment and put their backers on their boards.

Table I.1 summarizes the political, governmental, and attitudinal changes that have affected nonprofits over the past forty or so years.

Leadership Transitions

Not only were nonprofits evolving over the past four decades; leaders were evolving as well. As the task of running organizations changed over time, leaders constantly adjusted their sights and skills to keep up. Now, as these older leaders depart, many groups are preparing for their first generational shift in leadership. No longer will the familiar boomers and veterans of change who brought these organizations through so many transitions be at the helm. There will be a new generation of leaders, new staffers, and new board members who will have different ideas and experiences.

Table I.1.   Changing Influences on Nonprofit Organizations

1960s, 1970s	• Liberal views dominate • Emphasis on systems and policy change • Nonprofit organizations developing, full of possibilities • Activists entering nonprofits as paid workforce • Government's role seen to provide for those in need • Sector grows through government and other funding • Government held accountable for needs of the poor
1980s, 1990s	• Conservative views in ascension • Government role seen as the problem, not the solution • Cuts in funding for nonprofit groups; switch from grants to reimbursements • Nonprofits previously dependent on government money diversify funding sources • Challenges raised regarding the effectiveness of social change work • Nonprofits held accountable
2000–	• Reemergence of a vocal progressive opposition to the religious right • Deep distrust of government • Entrepreneurs on the rise; one person or idea can make significant change • Emphasis on nonprofit measurable outcomes, theory of change • Nonprofits seen as the problem, not the solution • Concern about the future of nonprofit organizations

Our Information

This book is designed to help you recognize the interests and needs of these new generations of leaders, understand the decisions facing aging leadership, and think about what type of leadership is needed for social sector work in the future. We have read hundreds of books and articles on generations and generational change in nonprofits, business, and government. We have conducted formal interviews with older and younger nonprofit leaders and younger staff members; convened generational and cross-generational focus and discussion groups with those in nonprofit leadership positions; and participated in thousands of individual and group conversations about generational changes in nonprofits. Our informants come from all over the United States and Canada. They work in predominantly small and midsized organizations and represent not only different age groups but also differences in race/ethnicity, gender and gender identity, immigration status, sexual orientation, educational background, and income groups. They work on a large range of issues in a variety of settings, from settlement houses to environmental justice groups, from educational programs to organizing low-income residents, from the performing arts to legal advocacy. We have listened, asked questions, and listened again.

We also draw on our own experiences, which cross lines of age and generation, race, gender, country of origin, class, religion, and family background. We work in different parts of the country, focus on different issue areas, and take different approaches. We have spent long days discussing, debating, and dissecting generational change and its meaning for nonprofit groups and social change work. We hope the fruits of that work will yield ideas and tools you can use during this period of transition and for the challenges we face in the future.

What's Ahead

Working Across Generations makes available information about leadership change, generations, and frameworks to help with transitions. Throughout, we provide stories, examples, and exercises that can be used by individuals and in group settings.

Part One offers a set of frames through which the future of nonprofit leadership can be viewed and provides the reader with the information about the different generations of social sector leaders. Chapter One reviews the studies that have raised both consciousness and anxiety about the exiting of the baby boom generation. We compare the older generation's fear that the social sector is facing a crisis as knowledgeable boomers leave with the perceptions of newer generations who worry about outdated organizations, undoable executive jobs, and little recognition of their ideas.

In Chapter Two, we present the generations: both who they are and how they differ, including how they view each other's work and legacy. Chapter Three addresses two frameworks, roles and values, that lay the groundwork for understanding different generations' leadership tasks and the way they build bonds as they work for a common vision, build trust, and come to a common awareness of the problems they are trying to solve.

Part Two turns to the different ways generations of social sector leaders view the future. In Chapter Four, we discuss boomers' thoughts and fears about how long they will stay in the social sector. The views of Generation X and the millennials are presented in Chapter Five, including their concerns about whether and how to lead nonprofit groups. The book concludes with an examination of how to communicate across generations and recommendations for future research and action.

Throughout the book, we have included many tables and exercises to present our concepts and engage the readers. Key tables and all the exercises in this book are also available from *www.workingacrossgenerations.org*. We hope you will find this additional resource helpful.

Notes

1. For a complete discussion of social change organizations, see Chetkovich, C., and Kunreuther, F. *From the Ground Up: Grassroots Organizations Making Social Change*. Ithaca: Cornell University Press, 2006.
2. Mannheim, K. *Essays on the Sociology of Knowledge*. London: Oxford University Press, 1952.

3. Brokaw, T. *The Greatest Generation*. New York: Random House, 1998; Gillon, S. *Boomer Nation: The Largest and Richest Generation Ever and How It Changed America*. New York: Free Press, 2004; Howe, N., and Strauss, W. *13th Gen: Abort, Retry, Ignore, Fail?* New York: Vintage Books, 1993; Howe, N., and Strauss, W. *Millennials Rising: The Next Great Generation*. New York: Vintage Books, 2000.

4. Filipczak, B., Raines, C., and Zemke, R. *Generations at Work: Managing the Clash of Veterans, Boomers, Xers, and Nexters in Your Workplace*. New York: AMACOM, 2001; Tulgan, B. *Managing Generation X: How to Bring Out the Best in Young Talent*. New York: Norton and Company, 1996; Carucci, R. *Leadership Divided: What Emerging Leaders Need and What You Might Be Missing*. San Francisco: Jossey-Bass, 2006; Deal, J. *Retiring the Generation Gap: How Employees Young and Old Can Find Common Ground*. San Francisco: Jossey-Bass, 2007; Lancaster, L., and Stillman, D. *When Generations Collide: Who They Are. Why They Clash. How to Solve the Generational Puzzle at Work*. New York: HarperCollins, 2002.

5. See, for example: Jayson, S. "Companies Slow to Adjust Work-Life Balance Concerns of Gen Y." *USA Today*, December 8, 2006; Martin, C. "Healing the Generational Rift in Feminism." [Weblog entry.] Huffington Post. June 12, 2007; Trunk, P. "What Gen Y Really Wants." *Time*, July 5, 2007; Broder, J. "Shushing the Baby Boomers." *The New York Times*, January 21, 2007; Jayson, S., and Puente, M. "Gen Y Shaped, not Stopped, by Tragedy." *USA Today*, April 17, 2007; Friedman, T. "Generation Q." *The New York Times*, October 10, 2007.

6. See http://www.aecf.org/knowledgecenter/publicationseries/executivetransitionmonographs; *GEO Action Guide: Supporting Next Generation Leadership*. Washington, D.C.: Grantmakers for Effective Organizations, March 2008.

7. Bell, J., Moyers, R., and Wolfred, T. *Daring to Lead: A National Study of Nonprofit Executive Leadership*. San Francisco:

CompassPoint Nonprofit Services and The Meyer Foundation, 2006; Boland, P., Jensen, C., and Meyers, B. *Addressing the Leadership Challenge: Non-Profit Executive Directors' Views on Tenure and Transition in Alberta*. Calgary, AB: Calgary Centre for Non-Profit Management, 2005; Ancrum, R., Liss, K., Maas, S., and Randall, G. *Executive Director Tenure and Transition in Southern New England*. Worcester, Mass.: Greater Worcester Community Foundation, 2004.

8. Solomon, J., and Sandahl, Y. *Stepping Up or Stepping Out: A Report on the Readiness of Next Generation Nonprofit Leaders*. Washington, D.C.: Young Nonprofit Professionals Network, 2007; Davis, E. "Young Nonprofit Professionals: Preparing the Path for Leadership." October 2007, http://www.edaconsulting.org; Cornelius, M., Corvington, P., and Ruesga, A. *Ready to Lead? Next Generation Leaders Speak Out*. Washington, D.C.: The Meyer Foundation, 2008.

9. Kim, H., and Kunreuther, F. *What's Next? Baby Boom-Age Leaders in Social Change Nonprofits*. New York: Building Movement Project, 2007; Tierney, T. "The Leadership Deficit." *Stanford Social Innovation Review*, Summer 2006; Masaoka, J. *The Departing: Exiting Nonprofit Leaders as Resources for Social Change*. Washington, D.C.: Grantmakers for Effective Organizations, 2007.

10. Brinckerhoff, P. *Generations: The Challenge of a Lifetime for Your Nonprofit*. St. Paul: Fieldstone Alliance, 2007.

11. Light, P. "The Content of Their Character: The State of the Nonprofit Workforce." *The Nonprofit Quarterly*, Fall 2002 (Vol. 9, Issue 3); "Winning the Talent War: New Brookings Survey Finds the Nonprofit Sector Has the Most Dedicated Workforce." Washington, D.C.: Brookings Institution, October 3, 2002.

12. Kerner Commission. *Report of the National Advisory Commission on Civil Disorders*. Washington, D.C.: U.S. Government Printing Office, 1968.

Part One

GENERATIONS OF LEADERS

1

WHICH CRISIS?

> There are some people who are lifers at the
> organization, and some who come and go within
> a couple of years. There's the old generation that's
> been there since the organization was founded,
> and there's the new generation that comes in,
> stays a couple of years and then leaves. Personally,
> I'm questioning how much longer I'm going to be
> involved—not because of my commitment to the
> community, but is there really an opportunity for
> me to make change there if the older generation
> isn't willing to give up some of that power; give us a
> real voice?
>
> *Generation Xer*

Most of the talk about generation change in nonprofit leadership refers to the exodus of aging baby boomers whose anticipated departure has created enormous anxiety in the sector. The
boomers are entering their sixties, an age that previous generations saw as a traditional time of retirement. That means the
organizations this generation founded and built will need to find
new executives to take their place.

But talk with a boomer, and the first thing he or she is likely
to say is, "I'm not going anywhere!" In our workshops and discussion groups, most boomers were more worried about becoming obsolete than finding a suitable replacement. They were
clear that they still had the energy, interest, and power to stay in
their positions. And they certainly had no intention of leaving

until they decided it was the right time to go. So what is happening? Are boomers ready to leave their jobs behind to take a much-needed rest as they enter their twilight years? Or is this large and energetic cohort gearing up for two more decades at the helm of nonprofit and social change work?

What Is the Crisis?

In 2001, a national study of nonprofit executive directors reported shocking results. Published by the California-based management support organization CompassPoint, *Daring to Lead* found that 75 percent of nonprofit executive directors planned to leave their jobs in the next five years.[1] The statistics were hard to ignore, especially when a series of follow-up studies confirmed their results. For example, a study of United Way of New York City grantees found 45 percent of executive director/chief executive officers planned to leave their positions within five years.[2] A national study commissioned by the Annie E. Casey Foundation reported 65 percent of nonprofit executives said they were leaving in the next five years.[3] In Alberta, Canada, 86 percent of nonprofit leaders surveyed stated they would leave their jobs within the next five years.[4] The University of San Diego found 68 percent of the area's nonprofit leaders expected to leave in the next five years.[5] And the New England Executive Transitions Partnership study stated that over 70 percent "imagined" they would leave their position within five years.[6]

It was demonstrated again and again in studies across the United States and Canada: executive directors were leaving, and the nonprofit sector was unprepared to handle their mass departure. To many it seemed obvious: the baby boom generation of leaders was aging, and retirement was just around the corner. Within a few years of the release of *Daring to Lead*, a new field, executive transition management (ETM), was developed to help nonprofit groups anticipate the impact of impending leadership transitions and support them through the process.[7]

The focus was not only on departing executives. Concerns about who would replace them gave new energy to initiatives designed to identify and train emerging leaders. There was also growing support for programs encouraging people to enter nonprofit work.[8] The emphasis was on grooming new talent who would be in the pipeline. They would be learning how to take on nonprofit leadership while aging executives prepared for their exit.

In 2006, another report, *The Leadership Deficit*, was published by Bridgespan, a nonprofit arm of the for-profit consulting firm Bain & Company. The report predicted there would be 640,000 vacant nonprofit senior management positions over the next ten years, more than double the number currently existing.[9] Using a statistical model based on the aging population and the figures on the number of new nonprofits that are formed each year, Bridgespan, with its corporate credentials, caught the attention of the nonprofit world, especially foundations. Where would the new leadership come from, and how was the sector going to survive?

A Closer Look

Although there was growing alarm about the retiring boomers, few people were questioning the conclusions that were being drawn from these studies. Why would they? There was plenty of work for those providing ETM services from organizations putting into place succession plans or in the midst of dealing with leadership change. Programs and fellowships for those interested in learning the skills needed to lead were full of energetic talent of all ages. There was clearly a need and certainly a problem that was necessary to address.

The release of *Daring to Lead 2006* was the clue that there was more to the findings. This next installment of the study again asked a representative sample of nonprofit executives in the United States about their future plans. Once again there was the dramatic finding: 75 percent of executive directors planned to leave their jobs within the next five years.[10] Yet surprisingly little attention was given to the fact that between the two reports, five years had elapsed and the predicted turnover had not occurred.

Why were so many studies finding that nonprofit executive directors were planning to move on even though they continued to stay? What were these leaders telling us? If CEOs were not leaving, what motivated them to keep saying it was time go? The answers lay squarely in the reports themselves and are confirmed in some of the observations made by the next generations.

The nonprofit leadership crisis, it turns out, is not simply about the baby boom generation aging out of jobs. Only 17 percent of directors in *Daring to Lead 2006* said they were planning to retire, a fact almost entirely overlooked by those pushing the crisis scenario.[11] Nor do those who say they will leave seem to want to pursue other interests outside the social sector. The vast majority want to continue working in nonprofits. It turns out that leaders don't want to retire or leave the sector; they just want to leave their jobs.

The anticipated exodus of nonprofit leaders—the one that still has not happened—is not about age; it is about the executive director position. Of course, the boomer cohort will start to step out of their job—and the nonprofit sector in the coming decades—but the focus on their exit has overshadowed how unhappy so many are in their current positions. Both *Daring to Lead* studies found that executive directors want to get out of their positions because of the amount of stress they experience on the job. Leaders find great pleasure in the impact their organizations have and the relationships they form with colleagues, but these rewards are outweighed by the unrelenting demand to raise funds, manage finances, and, in too many cases, work with unsupportive boards of directors. To meet these needs, executives work long hours with relatively low compensation. Even more disturbing is that nonprofit leaders worry not just about making ends meet but about the assessment of their work by their boards. *Daring to Lead 2006* found that one-third will be pushed out or fired before they voluntarily choose to walk out the door. Those leading larger and better-resourced organizations are significantly happier with the job, the pay, and the support they receive from both boards and funders. But most nonprofits are small to midsized groups, where leaders are responsible, often without much help, for keeping the doors open.

If the problem facing the sector is not that boomers are leaving, but that the demands of the work result in executives wanting to quit their jobs, then there are important implications for organizations and the sector as a whole. The analysis and assumptions we make about older leaders exiting and newer ones entering nonprofit organizations may be focused on the wrong issues.

Plans of the Next Generation

In our conversations with younger leaders, they rarely discuss the crisis of baby boomers leaving the sector. When they talk of boomer leaders and veterans of change, they are much more likely to notice the stress in older directors who have dedicated themselves to keeping their organizations alive. Generation Xers and millennials watch these older leaders with mixed reactions. On the one hand, many cannot imagine that they would ever want to be in a similar position. Heading a nonprofit organization appears to be a thankless job with enormous demands on the leader's time that leaves little room for the pleasures that program work offers. On the other hand, younger workers are discouraged that the help and relief they can offer older leaders frequently goes unrecognized. They feel the skills they bring to the work are often left untapped by older directors, who are used to doing it all themselves.

Some of the studies on nonprofit leadership help to explain these observations. For example, the United Way study in New York City asked directors to identify staff members they thought had the most leadership potential and then asked leaders whether these staffers were ready to take on the top role. Most of the boomer executives rated these potential leaders' skills far lower than this next tier rated themselves. Even if the older leaders were right in their assessments, they were reluctant, especially in small organizations, to offer development opportunities to this group, fearing it would result in their most talented employees leaving the organization.

A recent study by the membership group Young Nonprofit Professionals Network, which "engages and supports future nonprofit and community leaders," asked members about their future plans. Forty-five percent of the respondents reported that they will leave the nonprofit sector. The reasons most often mentioned were burnout, low salaries, lack of career advancement, and job-related stress.[12] But leaving now did not mean staying away. In fact, 60 percent of those planning to leave and 65 percent who want to stay say they expect to be a nonprofit executive director in the future. That's good news, except that many report that they "are ambivalent about taking on an executive director role," fearing its impact on their quality of life.

Younger generations are wary. If they stay in the sector, they can work in organizations with a social mission—where they can make a real difference—but they may have to sacrifice both time and money, and there is no guarantee they will advance to leadership jobs.

Redefining the Problem

So is the problem that boomers are exiting? Or is it that the executive director job is too stressful? Are there too few younger leaders to take on positions as older leaders retire? Or are younger leaders' skills left untapped by current CEOs? We suggest that there is no one problem that we are trying to solve. The studies reveal that the issue is more complex than we might have originally believed. What makes this time of transition both confusing and exciting is that it is multilayered. There are several ways to define the problem, and each leads to a different set of solutions.[13] To illustrate this, let's look at five ways to think of generational shifts in nonprofit leadership and the implications of each on the future of the sector.

Baby Boom Leaders Are Leaving

The most common scenario about nonprofit leadership is that the sector is facing a crisis because the baby boomers are aging and will soon leave their leadership jobs—*in droves*. This exodus will create a vacuum at the top and put nonprofit organizations and the entire nonprofit sector in peril. This scenario implicitly assumes that the problem is a people problem, that is, there are not enough people to take the jobs that will be vacated. The solution to this crisis is the *replacement theory*: if leaders are leaving, we need to find new ones to take their place. One person goes out and another comes in. We then develop a pipeline—a place of preparation where new leaders are given training and support. But a pipeline does not conjure up images of innovation or new ideas. It readies people to fill a spot and contains those waiting for their turn.

If the crisis is that baby boomers are leaving their jobs, the solution is to develop new leaders across different age groups and sectors. Some suggest targeting young M.B.A.s, others prefer a focus on recruiting college students to the social sector, and still others encourage retired for-profit executives to try their hand at nonprofit work. The skilled pool will increase, the jobs will be filled, and the sector will be saved!

No Room at the Top

Another view, especially from newer generations, does not see the problem as the boomers leaving; rather it is that the boomers are *not* leaving. They see a powerful generation living longer, staying healthier, and maintaining interest in both making a difference and making a salary. In this *staying on top* situation, boomers want to continue to be in charge, especially after years of building their organizations. In addition, they may need to keep, or at least see no reason to give up, their earning power.

If boomers are staying on top, then the problem is that there is no place for newer generations to run organizations, share their ideas, or define the future of the sector. Unless they start their own groups, they will remain a poor second to a boomer-dominated sector for years to come. The ideas and observations of the oldest will dominate, and younger generations' interest in nonprofit work will wane.

If this is the problem, the solution is to find ways that new generations with fresh views and youthful energy can make a meaningful impact on the sector's organizations and work. Boomers who are coasting will be helped to find places in the organization or in other nonprofits where they can still contribute while new generations lead. Others who are making a difference will be tapped for their thoughts on how to include new people in significant roles. Younger leaders will find positions of authority and responsibility to make a significant impact, and the sector will be saved!

It's the Position, Stupid!

A different take on the problem focuses on the role of the top executive. In this scenario, the crisis is that the position of executive director as it is currently conceived is no longer viable. What worked forty years ago will not hold up to new generations. The work has changed, the positions have grown, and the context has shifted.

What is needed is to *redefine the position*. This scenario calls for very different solutions. Here we need to look at why the job is not viable and how it could be redefined. It means searching for new models for structuring the work. There need to be changes in the culture, education of boards, and support for a new norm of what is expected from those in the top positions. It is a risky business; yet, like generational change, some of these shifts are already taking place. For example, we found several organizations run by younger leaders who had codirectors, flattened hierarchies, and different types of team approaches. These groups are trying to distribute the responsibilities of the executive position among a small group to lessen the pressures of the job and allow leaders to have more time away from work.

A focus on reworking the executive director position would mean that nonprofits would take untenable jobs and redesign them so they are attractive to new leaders. There would be less burnout and more enthusiasm, and nonprofits would be improved overall. The sector will be saved!

You Don't Know What You've Got 'til It's Gone!

Another way to look at the issue of leadership change is the *recognition problem*. Here, older leaders and boards are blind to a new generation of potential leaders right under their noses. Rather than focus on recruitment, the solution to the recognition problem is to turn inward and scan existing organizations to find and polish the hidden gems. Part of the issue for older leaders, whether paid staff or board members, is their image of how leadership looks. These mental models are extremely powerful and can obscure recognition of those who may be eager to begin learning and practicing leadership skills.

One of the biggest barriers to visibility is race. For some, this is a conundrum. Everyone talks about wanting to hire people of color, especially in social change work. So how is it that new leaders of color are not in line for top jobs? Here we come back to the mental models. As described in the following story, the images we hold of who will be a good and able leader are very powerful. The *Daring to Lead 2006* report found the percentage of executive directors of color has remained at 17 percent, even among new and younger leaders. Yet we know that the U.S. population is becoming more diverse. Something is deeply amiss.

Who Can Do the Job?

Susan had been heading Youth for Change for almost seven years when she was offered a year-long fellowship to develop her leadership skills. Her deputy director, Ann, generously offered to be an interim director while Susan was gone. Ann had worked for Youth for Change for four years and had extensive experience running programs for youth. She had a special connection to the youth based on her own background growing up in an African American family where resources were scarce. She was loyal to the organization and to Susan, but most important, she was loyal to the kids. When Susan took her leave, she was not sure whether she would return to Youth for Change. After all, a year was a long time to be away. But she worried that the board would not consider Ann executive director material. Susan knew how difficult it had been for her as a white woman to convince some of her male board members that she could raise money from corporate executives. Although the board would never admit it, Susan suspected they would worry that Ann's race and class background might not mesh with their large donor base. So Susan was surprised when halfway through her fellowship, she received a call from the board chair. He wanted to know how the fellowship was proceeding and whether she was still planning to return to Youth for Change. Sensing there was more to the call, Susan suggested they meet. It was then that the board chair confessed the board was excited by how well Ann had been received by donors and the success of her leadership. More money was coming in, and they were

> *impressed with her business-like style. He made it clear*
> *that he would gladly hold the job for Susan, but if she did*
> *not plan to return, he wanted to let Ann know that she*
> *was in line for the position. Soon after this meeting, Susan*
> *resigned, and Ann was appointed the new head of Youth*
> *for Change.*

Race is not the only barrier to recognizing new leaders. Many younger leaders experience their age as a significant barrier to overcome. They want to be acknowledged for their contributions and feel ready to take on new challenges. But older directors seem unwilling to acknowledge new leadership—partly because they are so busy, partly because they are stuck in their own mental models, and partly because they don't have the skills and support needed to help younger leaders advance in the field.

In this scenario, the problem is identifying, encouraging, and training younger leaders who already work in the nonprofit sector. Once they are visible and supported, they will be hired for nonprofit leadership positions. Then the sector will be saved!

Another Organizational Form Is Possible!

There is yet another way to define the problem. In this scenario, the way nonprofit groups are structured and operate is outdated. Recruits to the sector find decision making cumbersome and unappealing, and there is little support from boards or funders to make change. As a result, new leaders are reluctant to take on the top jobs in these organizations.

When the nonprofit sector experienced its wave of growth in the 1960s and 1970s, new leaders often adopted a kind of modified corporation structure. They had a hierarchy with lines of authority that resulted in a triangular structure (see Figure 1.1),

Figure 1.1.   Hierarchy with Input

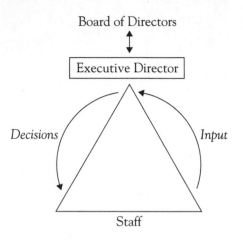

a common organizational form that was popular with the business sector at the time. The executive director was at the top, and staff fell in line underneath. To open up this top-down approach, non-profit directors sought input and feedback for their actions. They would listen to all the ideas and then make the final decision.

Yet somewhere along the way, as organizations grew and aged, this model started to become more bureaucratic. It took too long for information to flow up to the director. Staffers found their input unheeded and called for more transparency about the decision-making process. However, to this day, there are few alternatives, and even the smallest organizations adopt this model as they prepare for growth. As a result, new staffers yearn for what they imagine they could find in for-profit organizations that appear more flexible, open, and innovative. Executives would like to devolve more decision making but have trouble figuring out how to hold staff accountable for work when the bottom line in nonprofits is so often not clearly defined. In addition, accountability to the board and funders rests with the top leader, and that responsibility makes it difficult to let go.

If the problem is the organizational structure—the way decisions are made and the operations—then the solution is to reevaluate how the organizations are run and look for more suitable structures for the future. This is the *new structures and practices* solution. We should be researching and imagining how groups can operate in ways that will advance the sector's work, attract and support staff, and build new leaders. One approach would be to comb the for-profit literature, especially on small business, for examples that could be applied to nonprofit work, following the lead of many young social entrepreneurs. We could also look at models from both within and outside the United States and start to encourage and teach these new methods. There could be meetings with for-profit and nonprofit scholars to see if they can find ways to advance the field.

Addressing the questions about form with new structures and practices would result in organizations that are innovative, flexible, and fun to work in and lead. That would attract leaders to nonprofit work. The sector will be saved!

What Do We Do Next?

There is no magic bullet that will make generational shifts in leadership seamless, but these different scenarios show the many different aspects of the leadership transition that are contributing to anxiety about these changes. The challenge is to find a set of solutions that will address immediate and long-term needs.

This calls for our best thinking and most creative ideas. The social sector as a whole needs to be open to the new and think about the future in a way that is different from that of the past. Just as the way we frame the problem will define the solution, the attitude with which we approach these changes will certainly shape the outcomes.

Exercise 1.1, "Finding Leaders, Finding Solutions," is one way to engage a group in a discussion about the crisis in nonprofit leadership. (The exercise can also be modified as an individual reflection.) In the exercise, the group members (or the individual) identify what they see as the problems in finding new leaders. Then they look at personal, organizational, and structural solutions.

Exercise 1.1
Finding Leaders, Finding Solutions

This exercise can be used at a staff or board retreat or in work-shops for nonprofit leaders. We recommend using a facilitator to help keep the group on track and encourage people to move beyond their comfort zone. The exercise starts with a large group brainstorm, and then divides participants into small groups for discussion. The large group reconvenes for a report back and synthesis and ends with a discussion of next steps.

Step 1: Brainstorm

Start the exercise by asking, "What do you think are some of the problems facing the nonprofit sector in finding leaders?"

List responses on a flip chart.

Helpful hint: To help set the context for the exercise, ask participants to think about some of the challenges they have faced in their role as a nonprofit leader, when they try to take on more leadership, in making a decision about whether they would like to be a social sector leader. Here are some of the examples of problems we've raised in this chapter:

Problems Facing Nonprofits in Finding Leaders

1. Baby boomers are retiring, and there are not enough new leaders in the nonprofit sector to take their place.

2. Younger generations interested in nonprofit leadership have trouble breaking into high-level positions.

3. The top leadership position in nonprofits seems to be all work, no fun, and lots of sacrifice. Who would want those jobs?

4. Young leaders want (too) high salaries, and the sector cannot pay them enough.

5. Newer leaders don't have the training or skills to take on new leadership jobs.

Step 2: Cluster Responses

Organize the problems raised into clusters of similar issue areas. Transfer each cluster of problems on to separate sheets of flip chart paper, and post the clusters side by side.

Step 3: Small Group Assignment

Break into small groups by asking the participants to gather around the topics that they feel most drawn to. If there is a big imbalance among groups, ask some people to move to another issue they are also interested in.

Have the small groups take their list of problems and place them in different corners of the room. Provide flip chart paper and markers, and ask each group to choose a facilitator to keep time and a recorder.

Step 4: Small Group Brainstorm

Ask the participants in the small groups to brainstorm solutions to the problems posed. Push them to think creatively. Allow fifteen minutes, but extend the time if the groups are large. The recorder should write brainstorm suggestions on the flip chart paper for all to see.

After brainstorming solutions, each group reviews the responses.

Ask the group whether there is any variation in their responses by generation.

Then ask them to categorize each solution:

- Personal

- Organizational

- Structural

Some solutions may fall into more than one category. This part should be ten minutes.

Helpful hint: If the problem is that new potential leaders don't have enough training or skills to be executives, a *personal solution* would be for new potential leaders to seek out ways to build

(continued)

Exercise 1.1
Finding Leaders, Finding
Solutions (*continued*)

their leadership capacity. An *organizational solution* would be for the organization to start a training program for new potential leaders. A *structural or sectorwide solution* would be to make low-cost and effective training programs are made widely available.

Step 5: Reconvene the Large Group

Come back together as a large group, and ask each small group to report back on any generational differences. Then have them report on the personal, organizational, and structural solutions to the problems they were addressing. Have a recorder note their answers on separate flip chart sheets with these headings: personal, organizational, and structural solutions.

Have the facilitator ask the group to think about what steps are needed to implement these solutions on personal, organizational, and structural levels. This can be done first as an individual writing exercise or in small groups (with people from the same organization) with a report back to the larger group. Or it can be held as a large-group discussion.

Helpful hint: It might help participants if you structured the conversation by asking:

- What can people [or people in my organization] do to make these personal solutions to the problem of finding leaders possible?

- What can organizations [or my organization] do to implement these organizational solutions to finding leaders?

- What changes are needed in the nonprofit sector to implement these structural solutions to finding leaders?

Step 6: Report Back and Close

Report back to the full group the solutions that people came up with and see if there are personal and organizational commitments participants want to make before they leave.

Now that we have started the discussion on different views of the problem of nonprofit leadership, we turn to the generations. In the next chapter, we present information on how the different cohorts came to work for social change, their experiences in the sector, and their feelings about leadership and social sector work.

Notes

1. Peters, J., and Wolfred, T. *Daring to Lead: Nonprofit Executive Directors and Their Work Experience*. San Francisco: CompassPoint Nonprofit Services, 2001.
2. Birdwell, D. S., and Muzzio, D. *The Next Leaders: UWNYC Grantee Leadership Development and Succession Management Needs*. New York: United Way of New York City, 2003.
3. Teegarden, P. H. *Nonprofit Executive Leadership and Transitions Survey 2004: Milwaukee*. Baltimore: Annie E. Casey Foundation, 2005.
4. Boland, P., Jensen, C., and Meyers, B. *Addressing the Leadership Challenge: Non-Profit Executive Directors' Views on Tenure and Transition in Alberta*. Calgary, AB: Calgary Centre for Non-Profit Management, 2005.
5. Dietrick, L., and Creager, P. *Executive Transition in San Diego's Nonprofit Sector*. San Diego: University of San Diego, Center of Applied Nonprofit Research, 2006.
6. Ancrum, R., Liss, K., Maas, S., and Randall, G. *Executive Director Tenure and Transition in Southern New England*. Worcester: Greater Worcester Community Foundation, 2004.
7. See www.aecf.org/knowledgecenter/publicationseries/executive transitionmonographs. Other examples include www.supportctr .org, www.transitionguides.org, www.compasspoint.org.
8. Many of these programs were started before these studies were released. For information about leadership programs, see the Leadership Learning Community (www.leadershiplearning. org). Information on workforce development can be found at American Humanics Nonprofit Workforce Coalition www

.humanics.org/coalition). See also: Cryer, S. *The Nonprofit Career Guide: How to Land a Job That Makes a Difference.* St. Paul: Fieldstone Alliance, 2008.

9. Tierney, T. "The Leadership Deficit." *Stanford Social Innovation Review,* Summer 2006. The report's analysis excluded hospitals and higher education.

10. Bell, J., Moyers, R., and Wolfred, T. *Daring to Lead: A National Study of Nonprofit Executive Leadership.* San Francisco: CompassPoint Nonprofit Services and The Meyer Foundation, 2006.

11. To be fair, this was not the case in all of the studies. For example, in San Diego, almost two-thirds of those who anticipated leaving said they would like to retire.

12. Solomon, J., and Sandahl, Y. *Stepping Up or Stepping Out: A Report on the Readiness of Next Generation Nonprofit Leaders.* Washington, D.C.: Young Nonprofit Professionals Network, 2007. Respondents could answer more than once. Although they said they would leave nonprofit work, many indicated they would like to consult or work for a foundation, showing that they may indeed stay in the sector.

13. Thanks to Patrick Corvington for his help in developing these ideas.

2

MEET THE GENERATIONS

What do we really know about the different generations, and how does that knowledge affect the leadership of nonprofit organizations? Drawing on our interviews and focus groups, in this chapter we look at how older generations, especially baby boomers, came into social sector work, their contributions over the past four decades, and their views of the next generations. Then we turn to Generation X and the first of the millennial cohort, examining similar terrain as they take on social sector leadership.

Older Generations at a Crossroads

We all thought that change was permanent. It was so obvious; the revolution was coming.—Baby boomer

The greater generation. The largest and richest generation ever. Optimistic, affluent, and idealistic. These descriptions of baby boomers capture the power of this generation since the first articles on them grabbed the imagination of the U.S. population in 1948.[1] Over 78 million people born in the United States between 1946 and 1964, boomers are the daughters and sons of the World War II generation. They grew up in the 1950s and 1960s, a time of relative prosperity for the country and a growing middle class.[2] Their parents, noted for their loyalty and patriotism, were challenged by some of the ideas, culture, and styles of this new generation, whose early trademark was change.[3]

In this section, we look at some of the traits attributed to the boomers and late veterans of change, and see how these generations were influenced by the social justice movements of the 1960s and 1970s. These formative events led many to work for nonprofits, where they could continue to express their passion for social change.

Who Are the Baby Boomers, and What Defines Them?

The baby boom population is a study in contrasts.[4] Many were born and raised in postwar prosperity with increased living standards and suburban sprawl spawned by the G.I. Bill for returning veterans.[5] They were influenced by Martin Luther King Jr., Bob Dylan, Gloria Steinem, James Brown, Cesar Chavez, The Beatles, and Rosa Parks. Baby boomers were the first generation to grow up with television, which galvanized them around shared experiences. They sat with their families viewing the coverage of the civil rights marches, the assassination of President Kennedy, and the Vietnam War protests. Over the span of years that define boomers and the late veterans of change, they watched TV shows ranging from *Leave It to Beaver*, to *Soul Train*, to *The Brady Bunch*. Many were children of the new suburban middle class, but this generation also encompasses those who grew up in blue-collar families, worked in the fields as children of migrant laborers, struggled with poverty in large cities, or faced overt racism in schools and in their hometowns.

With their numbers and sense of self-importance, boomers are also seen as the original "me" generation. Their parents had been children of the Great Depression who held onto their frugality (and savings) and belief in the importance of hard work and playing by the rules. The baby boom generation, buoyed by the security of their parents, found themselves looking for individual freedom and self-expression. Rather than play by the rules, they wanted to transform them. They were dissatisfied with the expectations they had been given of gradual, incremental change, and they used their youthful zeal and sheer numbers to challenge the status quo.

The Baby Boom Generation and Social Activism

> To see the civil rights movement was a stunning thing for a person, sixteen. These were eye-opening experiences.—Baby boomer

Boomers we interviewed who are now leaders in the nonprofit sector often refer to the movement activities that took place during their younger years. Many also had earlier influences that made them fertile ground for social change work. For example, boomers and veterans of change talked about the role that religious tradition played in instilling lifelong social change values. One boomer said, "I felt I got grounding out of the Catholic Church where I was taught about faith, hope, love, and charity; but also about justice and responsibility."

We heard boomers speak of liberation theology, summer camps for children of progressive Jews, and religious activism, where they learned about colonial struggles outside the United States and inequality at home. Some of these activities resulted in early personal experiences related to the civil rights movement, such as witnessing the first school integration or going to Mississippi with a church youth group, that were life-directing events.

The need to fight for the rights of those with little power and influence also started in families. Boomers talked about growing up in a working-class or union household, being a "red-diaper baby" (that is, a child of parents who were members of the U.S. Communist party), or having a family who had fought for equality over generations. Class experiences motivated baby boomers too. One boomer saw activism and social change work as a way to escape from rigid class expectations:

> All I knew was I couldn't face rotating shifts at a factory. . . .
> I had this fixation on meaningful work because I grew up in a
> world where people didn't have meaningful work.

Those from low-income communities remembered how the daily struggles to survive drove them to challenge unjust and racist systems:

> I got to see a lot of injustices. I saw how we were treated as second-class citizens because we spoke Spanish . . . seeing my classmates have their mouths washed out with soap for speaking Spanish.

These early experiences were where baby boomers first understood the problems caused by inequality. But it was the social justice movements of the 1960s and 1970s that gave them the points of entry to make a difference.

The Movements. Contemporary movement building in the United States conjures up the mobilizations of the 1960s, starting with the civil rights movement and including free speech and antiwar activities; movements for women's, black, Chicano, indigenous, and Asian American rights; and gay liberation (now the lesbian, gay, bisexual, transgender movement). Many of the activists in the 1960s were involved in groups fighting for economic equality, building on a history of workers' rights and union struggles in the 1930s. There were sectarian groups seeking revolutionary restructuring of the economic system. Some people were committed activists; others watched from the sidelines, enjoying the new freedoms of the boomer generation coming of age. There were hippies who lived on communes, draft resisters who went to jail or fled to Canada, and druggies who were seeking an altered consciousness. For people who were politically involved and those who were not, these were touchstones of the baby boom generation, and they have taken on almost mythic proportions for those who participated in them and for younger activists who have followed.

The movement of this period created a sense that things could and would be different for this generation. It was a time of hope and possibilities. The boomer and veterans of change leaders we talked with often had engaged in sustained activism and enjoyed a shared identity, at least in hindsight. They worked hard, driven by political values that allowed them to envision a new, more just world. This was an exciting time to be young and politically active.

> The image then was we can change the world; we can have [an] impact to change society.

And change did happen, ranging from the passage of the Civil Rights Act to the end of the war in Vietnam. There was the establishment of National Welfare Rights Organization where people on welfare pressured government to move resources to underserved populations and to claim their own dignity and self-determination. Affirmative action programs offered educational and job opportunities to people of color. Community action agencies were founded across the country to bring together the public and private sectors with low-income communities to develop strategies to fight poverty. Women's consciousness-raising groups changed the way women saw themselves in relation to men and to society. This generation believed they were creating a new world, and transforming themselves in the process.

Transformation: Personal and Political. We noticed in the stories of the older generations of nonprofit leaders how they were personally changed by the movements of the time and how these transformations gave them a new lens through which to see the world. The political and social organizations they joined valued learning and consciousness raising, leading them to a new understanding of how decisions were made, power operated, and systems worked.

A Vietnam Radical

Jerome Scott, a longtime African American activist, said going to Vietnam radicalized him. When he was in Vietnam, someone asked him, "Why are you here?" The question startled him, but he offered his knee-jerk response: "They sent me." Yet the weight of that question shook him up. Jerome realized that he did not know why he was there. From then on, Jerome explains, "I pledged that I would never do anything or go anywhere unless I knew why."

When he returned to Detroit, he looked for ways to channel his political activism. He became involved in organizing autoworkers and participated in the League of Revolutionary Black Workers. He then moved to Atlanta to work with the Equal Rights Congress. In 1986, he founded Project South: Institute for the Elimination of Poverty and Genocide because he wanted to emphasize and amplify the strategic role of the South in the struggle for justice in U.S. society. Project South was one of the key organizers of the first United States Social Forum in 2007, where over twelve thousand young and veteran activists gathered to share their work and develop alliance-building strategies for large-scale change.

Certainly not every baby boomer or veteran of change we spoke with had been an activist in this period. Yet they all noted that they had been altered by the times. They had witnessed large changes in a relatively short period, and it gave them a sense of efficacy and power. There were new attitudes and visible differences: desegregation of public schools, more people of color with college degrees, women engaged in paid and meaningful work, gays and lesbians coming out, liberation movements across the globe freeing themselves from colonial rule, among many others, and it seemed as if the changes would never end.

Building Infrastructure for Social Change

As the boomers shifted from young activists to breadwinners, they had a particularly strong influence on the development and growth of the nonprofit sector. As a result of their activities, significant amounts of government money became available to address problems of poverty and marginalization. These funds helped groups make significant inroads into needed change. Money was available for a range of activities—to build affordable (and livable) housing, establish rape crisis hotlines, create new youth programs, open day care centers, and form new advocacy groups.

It was in nonprofit organizations that boomers could dedicate themselves full time to work for social change, and they still express surprise that they were able to parlay their activism into jobs. One boomer recalled her first paid movement position: working for reproductive rights. In spite of her marginal salary, she felt lucky that she could be employed in doing the work that meant so much to her and her fellow activists.

Money also went to service groups, new and old, to address the immediate needs of distressed communities. Pressure on local government to redirect funds to local communities resulted in the devolution of programs to nonprofit organizations who believed they could do a cheaper and better job than bureaucratic public agencies. Boomers interested in change also joined unions, worked for government, or went into the business sector. Some look back on their early years as youthful zeal, but most still believe that they made a real difference.

Building the Organization, Developing into Leaders. Gordon Chin is the founding executive director of San Francisco's Chinatown Community Development Center. He has been in his position since 1977, after eighteen different jobs to support himself through college and his activist work. The center finally gave him the opportunity to work full time for the community. He now oversees an organization with fifty-five staff members working on issues ranging from affordable housing to tenant services to community planning, while still including advocacy and organizing. Chin is proud that his generation made full-time activist work possible for himself and many others. His current work may not be as exciting as the marches and rallies of the 1960s and 1970s, but baby boom and veterans of change leaders regrouped in thousands of community organizations and dug in their heels for the long haul. They are still determined to make a significant contribution to the building of the movement infrastructure.

Since there was no blueprint for turning their activism into long-term, full-time careers, most baby boom leaders were not prepared for managing and developing nonprofit organizations. Undeterred, they improvised and learned along the way. They talk about their commitment to building organizations that reflected their political values of equality and fighting injustice. Ellen Gurzinsky, a longtime activist and former director of a progressive foundation, explained, "We lived our politics. I think that we put a lot of time into founding organizations and building organizations that reflect our politics."

Learning by doing has been the modus operandi for boomers and veterans of change, and they carry that spirit with them to this day. It has meant developing their leadership by trial and error. We repeatedly heard from the older generations that they did not set out to lead organizations, but grew into leadership as a result of the job and their determination to keep working for change. "I was never prepared to take on the leadership roles I did," said one boomer. "None of us had a clue what we were getting ourselves into."

These boomers channeled their passion, hard work, and can-do attitude to build their organizations. To them, this was not a job or a career. It was their life.

Older Generations: Back to the Future. The social change makers who entered nonprofits were challenged in the final two decades of the twentieth century when the conservative turn in the United States stifled movement momentum and made organization building even more of an imperative. Some groups failed as a result of government cuts in funding, but others grew through the acumen of their now-experienced leadership and pressure from communities.

Nevertheless, the past decades have taken their toll. While boomers scrambled to save their gains in areas such as civil rights, the environment, access to health care, affordable housing, and quality public education, they watched the optimism so prevalent in the 1960s and 1970s fade. Boomer leaders of organizations find themselves in multifaceted and demanding executive director positions. They are fundraising in an increasingly competitive environment, supervising staff, overseeing complex financial arrangements, managing boards that want meaningful input, and responding to ever-changing demands for accountability. One director commented, "The more successful we are, the more paperwork [we have], and it's killing me."

Many boomer executive directors, especially of larger organizations, mention that they miss being involved in the content of the work. But those in small organizations often fare no better. They struggle with fulfilling administrative responsibilities and overseeing the programs. One baby boom director of a small nonprofit describes the toll it has taken to meet funders' changing priorities:

> I'm getting less patient with having to do so much administrative work. I don't want to write grants anymore, and I don't want to follow the budget. . . . I'm really tired of kissing the ass of rich people who don't know what they're talking about. Some of them do, but many of them don't and you can't tell them. I'm really tired of the panhandling.

Yet it is not always easy for boomers to hand tasks over to new staff. Older executives recognize that they need to teach and transmit what they know to other, often younger leaders in their organizations. But learning by doing has left them unprepared for systematically transferring knowledge and skills, exacerbating the problem of work overload and concentration of job responsibilities at the top. "The problem," noted one boomer, "is that our jobs have grown with us, but I have a hard time teaching others how to do it because I don't know how to do it; I just get it done somehow."

On a personal level, many baby boom leaders are weary of the administrative and fundraising part of the work, even if they are still energized by the mission of the organization.

> To tell you the truth I'm tired and I find myself having to work harder. I go in to work earlier and earlier. . . . I'm more and more frustrated.

They would like more time to focus on their own interests, whether on the job or elsewhere. Some boomers and veterans of change are ready to cut back if they can find a way to make doing so financially viable.

The exhaustion is due not only to administrative workload. After decades of frontline organizing, one baby boom director/ organizer said, "There comes a time when your nerves can't take it anymore."

It turns out that the older generations' success in building strong nonprofit organizations is a double-edged sword. They have maintained their commitment to social change work, but there has been an erosion of their enthusiasm as a result of years of attacks by the conservative right. When asked about the accomplishments of their generation, boomer leaders we talked with often reminisced about the exciting days in the 1960s and 1970s. The power and possibility of that time remain crystal clear to them. They all but ignore the hard work that has gone into making the nonprofit infrastructure that grew out of their early activities. The years of digging their heels in and trying to make sustainable change, often under politically difficult circumstances, have left many long-term directors longing for their days in the streets when the revolution was just around the corner.

How Baby Boom Generation Leaders View the Next Generation

One reason it is hard for boomers to let go is their unease about what will happen when they leave their organizations. Many have high regard for younger generations. They talk about younger leaders' breadth and depth, interest in social justice, and expansive outlook unlimited by, and perhaps untested by, the kind of experience that tends to constrain older leaders' vision and strategies. Older generations see younger leaders as much more adept at using technology to frame and move the issues. And they caution their peers not to be dogmatic in their views about what it means to work for social justice.

Some boomers believe that the new generations have a healthier approach to doing long-term, sustainable change work and recognize that their own assumptions about working long hours can be a path to burnout. In this comment, one boomer's positive feelings reveal the struggles with terms that are being set by a new generation:

> They [younger leaders and staff] are not thinking of working 24/7 in their jobs like I did. . . . I think there is a chance of people coming out healthier, more whole and having a more holistic relationship with the world around them. I think there's a little resentment that gets played out on both sides. I sometimes feel it, like people in my office don't want to work as hard.

Several baby boom generation leaders reject what they see as the myth that older generations, especially those who participated in the movements of the 1960s and 1970s, are more collectively oriented than newer ones. These boomers freely call their cohort the "me" generation, one that in the end supported charismatic leaders over a team or group approach. In comparison, the next generation of leaders seems less ego oriented and better able to work across traditional organizational and political divides:

> They don't bring like this ego-centered leadership, "I am the leader and you're disrespecting me." . . . I don't know how to explain it, but that's not one of their avenues for solving that. It's more like consensus building in that sense.

In addition, many boomers and veterans of change realize that they need to partner with younger generations in planning and implementing leadership transitions. One boomer leader said, "If you are not thinking about your own transition, you are not developing the next generation of leaders." For them, it is both a matter of organizational survival and self-interest. Many baby boom leaders are looking for ways to continue social change work even after they leave their current organization. Building relationships across generations may offer opportunities for older generations to contribute once they leave their formal positions.

What Gap? Some baby boom generation leaders doubt whether a generation gap exists and wonder if the focus on generation change is simply a distraction from the work of social change. They point out that differences that are often assumed to be generational may be simply differences in strategies. For example, one boomer noted that younger leaders' better understanding of technology can result in a program or approach that looks different but is basically the same. Another commented that in organizing, the old-school way of doing outreach is through door knocking and intermittent media coverage. Today's younger generations are able to reach a much broader public through new-media technology. In this way, they have a better chance of reframing the public debate on contentious issues. This boomer insists that the difference here is not generational but the mastery of new tools.

Generational Concerns

Older leaders who respect new generations still can find that it's hard to take that leap of faith that the next generations can fill their leadership roles. We often heard boomers complain that younger generations are too eager to be in charge, contributing to an existing level of distrust and fear about leadership transfer. Although many boomers took on leadership at a young age, they note that leadership jobs now require more training and experience than when they started decades ago.

Older leaders worry that rather than gaining the experience needed to be effective, new generations want to lead now and dismiss boomers' suggestions to wait and learn before taking leadership roles. Several baby boomers expressed doubts about whether the next generation of leadership has the interest or spirit needed for these jobs. And some are concerned that boomers' commitment to make life easier for their children resulted in a new generation that is materialistic and not willing to "pay their dues": "Young people want it now, but don't do much to get it. Get them to understand it doesn't come easy, doesn't come quick. . . . You have to earn it. . . . Success doesn't come on a silver platter."

Others thought that younger leaders' class aspirations may make them leave the nonprofit sector or abandon smaller community-based organizations:

> In this society, they are constantly bombarded with materialistic things. . . . You'll find that working for a grassroots organization will not fulfill your material needs. There is not that high compensation. And we all know that. So when you come with those realities . . . the next generation who have been bombarded more than we have, because when I grew up, I never had a television. . . . That's why I say working for a movement organization takes a lot of commitment and also practice.

Despite the mixed views boomers have of the new generations, they also want to know how to bridge the gap so they can preserve their life's work and support new leaders to do their best.

The Newer Generations: After the Boom

> Those of us who are younger sit around and talk about how these leaders are stuck in old paradigms. Their view of the future is taking us from 1963 to the 1980s. And here we are wondering when we will be able to address the world we live in now.—Generation Xer

Douglas Coupland's novel *Generation X,* now almost two decades old, created a sensation with its description of the post–baby boom generation struggling under the sheer numbers and influence of the generation that preceded them.[6] Portrayed as well educated, underemployed, and emotionally lost, the Xers in Coupland's novel suffer from lack of direction and meaning in their lives. Coupland's work marked the beginning of a proliferation of books, magazine and newspaper articles, Web sites, and discussions devoted to generational differences. Gen Xers were slackers, materialistic, independent, technologically savvy, comfortable with diversity, distrustful of traditional institutions, scarred by working or divorced parents, and committed to friends, not jobs.[7]

It is this generation that is stepping up to take over social change organizations, followed closely by their younger millennial siblings. In this section, we present the background and views of Generation Xers and of the early millennials in social sector work.

Up Next and Already at the Plate: Generation X and Millennials

Generation X has the dubious distinction of following the optimistic, dominant baby boom cohort. While the boomers basked in their accomplishments, Xers looked for their place in a world that had hunkered down to face the life that is, not the life that was imagined. They are the generation of the first Clinton years, Jerry Falwell's Moral Majority, and the ascension of Bill Gates. Race dominated the airways not through civil rights marches but in the O. J. Simpson trial and the Los Angeles riots after the police were acquitted of beating Rodney King. Dramatic change was happening outside the United States: the end of apartheid in South Africa, the fall of the Berlin Wall, and the mobilization of peoples across the globe fighting together for issues ranging from fair trade policies to land rights.

Xers are characterized as realists. They were influenced by Tupac Shakur, Air Jordan, Madonna, the Brat Pack, and the Cure. While they grew up, the suburbs had turned from sites of safety to pockets of alienation, so clearly depicted in the movie *The Ice Storm*. Generation Xers are children of divorced parents and working mothers, when economic security was no longer the norm. *Cosby* and *Family Ties* gave way to *Seinfeld* and *Friends*. Xers had goth, grunge, and rap. Race, gender, and sexual orientation turned from rigid identity categories to flexible markers where people crossed lines in new ways.

The millennials are still emerging, but as the oldest move through their twenties, these children of boomers (who are called the most child-centric parents ever) are seen as confident and idealistic, and already in positions where they are making an impact. This generation is distinguished by combining the hopefulness of the boomers and the realism of Xers. They have been growing up after the United States was rocked by 9/11 and as the world has become newly focused on terrorism, war, and instability. Yet many have grown up in families that have given them a sense of security and well-being.

Millennials are the first generation of technological natives. Their relationships are built on texting, MySpace, and Facebook. Entertainment comes live, but iPods are a must, with constant updates that travel anywhere. Millennials may watch *American Idol*, but they are also glued to YouTube and video games, all the while multitasking to keep up with their highly scheduled calendars.

The millennials are heavily divided by class. Diversity by race and ethnicity is more the norm, and yet they are part of the largest economic divide in over a century. For some, politics is shaped by study abroad, while others experience it personally as targets of anti-immigrant policies.

Generation Xers and the millennials came of age when the baby boomers were settled in their institutions and the fight had moved from the streets to the policy arenas. It is no surprise that these younger generations have different ideas about how the world operates and the role of nonprofit social change work.

New Generations in Nonprofit Work: The Draw

Generation Xers and millennials, like their boomer predecessors, enter social change activities influenced by personal experiences. Some talked about having suffered or witnessed violence, faced discrimination, or grown up without economic resources. Others were raised in families where social justice values were deeply ingrained, and from an early age, they wanted to do something to make the world a better place. There were Next Geners who learned about inequity through being challenged by friends or teachers to reexamine their assumptions and beliefs. We also heard from those who were looking for a way to express their values or religious beliefs. They were drawn to the ideals of social change work and the opportunity to make a difference.

But without large-scale movements to support them, it was often difficult to find a way to make a mark. Many had no idea there were organizations that had jobs where they could continue their early activism. Their friends were going into business for money-making opportunities in financial institutions and high-tech ventures, or in low-level positions that paid the bills while they pursued other interests. College graduates were heavily recruited into positions as corporations flocked to college campuses. Some fulfilled their dreams, or family expectations, by going to medical or law school. With little information about or support for social sector jobs, few knew that they could make a career doing good work.[8]

Yet new generations interested in addressing issues of inequality or injustice found their way to the sector. For example, one Xer was a premed student when he took a class that introduced him to a community-based organization in a neighborhood with few health services. He decided to volunteer in the children's program and became hooked on the work. As the first U.S.-born child in an immigrant family, he was on a mission to get his medical degree, and he had no idea there was a nonprofit sector. When he graduated, he decided to take a year off between college and medical school to head an organization that matched students interested in health care with nonprofit health groups in low-income areas.

College service-learning programs and semesters spent working for change in other counties are frequently mentioned as a way Generation Xers and millennials are introduced to social sector jobs. Next Geners have been inspired by their participation in community groups such as youth organizing or recreation programs, and some commit to short stints in Xer-founded social ventures such as Teach for America or City Year. The advent of Action Without Borders/Idealist.org, a global clearinghouse of nonprofit and volunteering resources, plus job listings and campus job fairs, has vastly improved exposure to the field.[9]

Personal Transformation. Unlike the boomers, Generation Xers and millennials generally do not refer to their personal transformation as the reason they decided to work in the social sector, and when transformative experiences do take place, they often happen on the job.[10] For example, one Generation X staffer in a collective for low-income women had a powerful experience at work when she learned about the history of welfare in the United States and realized that being poor was not her fault. She contrasted this transformational moment with a college program that taught low-income women community organizing:

> I think it's good to learn about organizing and it's good to do things in the community, but it's also important to understand the history and root causes. . . . There's more than just being in the community. There's also an understanding of how things got to be this way.

Skills to Lead

Once in the sector, Generation Xers talk about how difficult it is to find leadership positions in existing organizations. They are entering groups without the years of experience that boomers and veterans of change have accumulated, yet they want to do serious work. They note that the simple fact of growing up in the postmovement period makes their values, abilities, and motivations suspect to some boomer leaders. Having missed that experience, they look for ways to legitimize their ability to take on responsibility and authority.

A Good Education. Social change organizations may not be recruiting students on college campuses, but newer generations, especially Generation X, are relying on school to give them an edge. There are a range of possibilities now available to learn how to lead in nonprofit groups. Roseanne Mirabella has been tracking nonprofit management and leadership programs in the United States and found that in 2001, more than 250 colleges and universities offered courses related to leading nonprofits, and 114 programs have degrees or concentrations in nonprofit management.[11] Younger generations are taking advantage of these and other graduate programs in policy, public management, business, or law that can lead to higher-level social sector jobs—for example:

> I've added to my skills and education. I have commitment to growing and enhancing the sector, and it is going to be up to us to improve the sector's legitimacy and credibility. . . . We

have opportunities and learnings that the boomers didn't have. They didn't have nonprofit management programs and professional certifications. Although some in the field are skeptical of these degrees, others believe it gives new generations a needed edge.[12]

Education on nonprofit management addresses what boomer leaders note as the sector's increasing complexity. These programs provide new generations with information on supervision, financial administration, incorporation laws, ethics, and the rules and regulations that come with running and funding a nonprofit. But as it turns out, skills alone do not always lead to leadership positions.

Elite Matters. In our 2002 study, *Generational Change in Leadership: Implications for Social Change Organizations*, it turned out that all but one of the Generation X leaders had a degree from an elite college or university.[13] They were selected for the study based on the organizations they led; only later, during the data analysis, did we recognize that attending a well-known school seemed to inspire trust from older leaders and investment from funders. One young founder was clear that this connection had proved instrumental in his work. He started his organization while still a college student and readily acknowledged that going to Harvard, rather than attending a state school, gave him access to people and opportunities that would otherwise be unavailable.

The Business of Organizations. Contrary to the boomers, Generation X and the millennials in social change organizations do not shun the for-profit sector. These younger generations are far more likely to have worked in business or have friends and colleagues in for-profit jobs. They are comfortable turning to business books about innovation and leadership to give them ideas for their work, such as *Good to Great* or *The Tipping Point*.[14]

In fact, 78 percent of the respondents in *Ready to Lead* had worked in the corporate sector.[15] Generation Xers' experience in for-profits often brought with it an appreciation of the management and financial skills needed to run organizations.

The fluidity between sectors has increased as the for-profit sector retools its image from making money to making change, whether it is in social investing or green jobs. Even those who want to stay in the social sector can see for-profits as offering opportunity. The Young Nonprofit Professionals Network found 45 percent of the respondents planned to switch to the for-profit sector, with almost 70 percent reporting lack of career advancement among the top reasons they wanted to leave nonprofit work. More than half saw themselves returning to nonprofits in a leadership role later in their career.[16]

Leaving and Coming Home

John heads an organizing group in the community where he grew up. In fact, he laughs telling us about his experiences as a youth leader in the organization he now heads. Back then, John thought leadership meant getting his own way. He describes starting a youth program when he became interested in reading political history with his peers. But he was challenged by other youth who wanted a place to socialize, not study. With guidance from older staff members, John quickly found out that leading meant listening to what others have to say, even when they do not agree with you. His early experiences taught him valuing others' views was an important aspect of making social change.

After high school, John left the community to attend a prestigious college. There he was selected to be in a business leadership program for students of color and was immediately placed in a corporate sector position after graduation. John describes his experience in the for-profit

> *world as being as valuable as his early organizing training.*
> *He saw no conflict between this work and his social justice*
> *values. In fact, given his relatively young age, he was quite*
> *sure that he never would have been recruited for or been*
> *able to run his current organization without his business*
> *experience.*

As Generation Xers age, the millennials are starting to figure out their work trajectory. Some plan to return to school after a couple of years on the job; others are happy in their current positions. Watching those just a few years older starting ventures such as YouTube and MySpace, millennials, like Gen Xers, are thinking about how to apply these successes to social sector work.

One challenge is for millennials and Xers who lack a college degree. Recognized for their smarts, experience, and knowledge of the community, they often are hired to work in social change organizations and other nonprofits to address the needs of their own community. However, these groups are not always clear about how to support the advancement of community staff members. Some, like John, go on to college and return to take on leadership roles. Others stay in the community and may find there is little room to move up in the organization or the field. If community members are interested in being future leaders in social change groups, they, and those working in the sector, will need to be clear about how they will develop the skills needed to be successful in these positions.

The Commitment

I'm always trying to fight the system, so to speak, but I'm really being able to utilize my time, my energy toward something that is making the world a better place.—Millennial

Studies predict that Generations X and Y will hold far more jobs in their lifetime than the boomers and other older generations.

Yet many of those we talked with felt a deep commitment to their organization and were relieved to find a place where they can be with others who share their vision of the world. Some see their colleagues as family; others enjoy the comfort of the working partnerships they have developed. One millennial told us,

> It feels like it's a real privilege to be able to do a lot of the stuff that I do. . . . I can't think of another job right now that would really have all the elements that I have. So, I don't have a lot of motivation to leave at the moment.

It is not their lack of commitment that motivates newer generations to move on; it is because of it. For Generation X and the millennials, commitment is focused on the work, not the organization, even when they are in a position they love. Most staffers we talked with, even the one quoted in the previous paragraph, did move on to school, other positions, or new parts of the country. Their decisions to leave are more likely to be based on where they are in their life cycle and opportunities for advancement. Younger generations move on to obtain needed credentials, take positions that increase their leadership responsibilities and pay, and try their hand at starting their own organizations. Millennials are looking for interesting opportunities, and Generation X staffers are having families and planning for a future that might require more income or more time at home, or both.

Younger executive directors, especially founders, have a harder time than their staffers imagining a time when they would give up their positions. Some talked about how they ought to have a plan to move on for the sake of the organization, but they seem to be thinking of a transition that would take place decades ahead. Most were happy in the organization they were building and in a challenging job. One founder explained, "The reason I stayed here nine years is because my job constantly evolves and it's always something new. There has honestly not been a day I've not loved my job."

Personal Challenges for Next Generation Leadership

Every book and article on Generation X and millennials refers to the contrasts between them and the boomers in the way they see the divide between their work life and their personal life. They report that older generations live to work, and younger ones work to live. Despite this stereotype, this theme was consistently raised by younger generations.

Life Cycle and Flow. One reason Next Geners in nonprofits emphasize the need for time away from the job is their age. The oldest millennials, now in their mid-twenties, are happy in their jobs and often put in long hours. Coworkers can be friends, making the job even more important. But millennials also want to spend time with these and other friends outside of work, and have the freedom to engage in additional activities. They also are at an age when they are figuring out whether to go back to school, leave the sector, travel, explore different interests, or change jobs.

Generation Xers are in a different period in their lives: they are starting a family or committing to a career. Those with young children are constantly juggling to find family time, see friends, and still be on top of the job. Several studies have noted that Generation X men are more involved in child rearing, something that boomers aspired to but had more trouble accomplishing.[17] One Gen Xer told us, "I have a brand-new baby. I was used to solving problems by coming in two hours earlier and staying two hours later. Well, that won't work anymore."

Gen Xers without children also talk about the importance of spending time with family and friends. Time away from the job, even with colleagues, refuels them to meet the demands of the work.

The Increase of Work. Generation Xers and millennials, as well as boomers, are also coping with increased time on the job. Studies show that U.S. workers now put in longer hours than those in any other industrialized country except South Korea.[18] Technological advances mean that almost everyone is more accessible at all times, even on vacation, and e-mail and cell phones mean there is more to manage. Generation Xers and millennials may take time away from work for other activities, but they are often plugged in—available to the office without a physical presence.

Younger directors and many of the young staff members we interviewed are putting in long hours and talk about the importance of work in their lives. But they are less likely to see work as their life. They are less conflicted than their older peers with having a strong commitment to the job and spending time away from it. In this way, and others, they distinguish themselves from the boomer generation.

Leading After the Boom: Admiration and Awe

Although the popular literature often portrays Generation X as rejecting the social change attitudes that boomers embraced in their youth, we heard admiration for those who lived during and fought in these earlier movements for change. Younger leaders are fascinated by a time when people took enormous risks and made huge strides toward justice and equality.

They are in awe of the number and types of groups that existed and the goal of long-term systemic change. Many Xers and millennials seek out the history and talk about the influence of the work of older generations in inspiring them, especially during less optimistic times. And some have activist experience with boomers. In the 1980s and 1990s, older generations often worked side-by-side with new generations interested in social change on all kinds of issues: the HIV/AIDS epidemic, environmental justice, antiapartheid and divestment, antisweatshop and the promotion of fair labor standards.

In fact, younger generation leaders have no problem giving boomers and veterans of change their due. They recognize the older generations' commitment, years of experience, hard-fought wins, and perseverance in difficult times. Xers and millennials are clear about the benefits they received from these early battles, such as access to education, jobs, mobility, or more equity. The newer generations have heard and learned about what boomers accomplished, but now they want to find out what went wrong.

What Happened?

While younger leadership is interested in stories of personal transformation, details of victories, and evidence of change, they are even more curious to hear what they term "the real story": why certain groups refuse to work together, what strategies were failures, and, most of all, what happened within the movements that contributed to the dismantling of the older generations' progress to change the world. They often express frustration that boomers are quick to point out how great those times were but slow to respond to questions about the intervening years. One Xer told us,

> There needs to be a deromanticizing of the experiences of the civil rights movement—an education and honest conversation between those who went through it and the rest of us who did not. We need to be realistic about the expectations of what we can do. To be prepared for the long haul.

To make matters worse, younger generations often feel that they have received the blame for the retrenchment of the 1980s and 1990s, even though many were too young even to be conscious of the rollbacks. They hear boomers accuse their generation of not "taking up the work." One young social change leader confided that she and her friends chafed at the boomers' pride in their past. Instead, she said, they see the current state of the world as their inheritance from the boomers, who refused to acknowledge that they were unable to arrest the country's rightward shift.

Understanding Each Other

Understanding the differences among generations starts with listening to what each generation has to say about what shaped them, what is meaningful to them, and what they think will be helpful to others. One place to start is with Exercise 2.1. It asks you to identify important events in your past, note the personal impact, assess your (and your generation's) accomplishments and disappointments, and think about what would be useful to share with other generations.

We filled in some dates and events but you will want to put in others that are relevant to you and your work across generations. The information can be shared within generations and across them, starting the conversations we all need to have.

Exercise 2.1
What Are My Personal and My Generation's Accomplishments and Lessons?

Step 1

Review the Key Events for each decade. These are intended as a helpful guide for you to reflect on the important events over the past several decades. Add other historical events that were important to you.

Step 2

Answer the questions for each decade.

Step 3

Review your responses, and then answer the questions about how to share these experiences with others.

Key Events in the United States, by Decade

1960s

- Student Nonviolent Coordinating Committee
- United Farm Workers and the grape boycott
- Free speech movement
- Assassination of Martin Luther King Jr., John F. Kennedy, Robert Kennedy, and Malcolm X
- Stonewall rebellion

Accomplishments:

Challenges and Disappointments:

What Would Be Helpful to Share with Other Generations:

1970s

- *Roe* v. *Wade*
- Vietnam War
- Central American Solidarity
- Affirmative action

Accomplishments:

Challenges and Disappointments:

What Would Be Helpful to Share with Other Generations:

(continued)

Exercise 2.1
What Are My Personal and My Generation's Accomplishments and Lessons? (*continued*)

1980s

• Berlin Wall falls

• Immigration Reform and Control Act

• Antiapartheid movement

• HIV/AIDS

• Your other key events

Accomplishments:

Challenges and Disappointments:

What Would Be Helpful to Share with Other Generations:

1990s

• Americans with Disabilities Act

• North American Free Trade Agreement passes

• Welfare reform

• Antisweat-shop campaigns

• Your other key events

Accomplishments:

Challenges and Disappointments:

What Would Be Helpful to Share with Other Generations:

2000s

• World Trade Organization demons-trations

• 9/11 terrorist attacks

• War in Iraq and Afghanistan

• Hurricane Katrina

• Your other key events

Accomplishments:

Challenges and Disappointments:

What Would Be Helpful to Share with Other Generations:

Debriefing Questions

- What key events and experiences that have influenced you stand out?

- In what ways have they shaped how you view the world and how you approach your work?

- What would be helpful for others to know to better understand you? How would you share your story?

What We Want from Each Other

The wariness between generations can simply be about what they feel, or fear, they are not receiving. We end this chapter with a look at what older and younger generations committed to social change want from one another.

What Younger Generations Want

Gen Xers and millennials acknowledge that their generations and the times are different. Although they enjoy learning from boomers, they also have views, skills, and experiences they feel are more relevant to the world today. Global capitalism, technology, more diversity, worldwide unrest, and the increasing gap between rich and poor all influence how new generations see the social sector and ways to lead.

Younger generations want older social change leaders to:

- Provide information and advice based on their experience that will help younger leaders be more effective in building future social change.

- Acknowledge younger generations' leadership, ideas, and vision.

- Share power and recognize that newer generations will be leading social change in the future.

Younger generations admire boomers and veterans of change and know there is a lot to learn from them. Older leaders deserve time to reminisce about the good old days, but they will help newer generations to lead when they are reflective about their past, passing on important lessons. Boomers need to start recognizing the leadership qualities and vision of Generation Xers and millennials, even when their styles and approaches differ from their own. And it's time to learn how to share power.

What Older Leaders Want from the Next Generations

Boomers and veterans of change need to make room for new leadership, but in many cases, they do not know exactly what that means. Boomers are not planning to retire in any traditional way, and they have the knowledge, experience, and stamina to go on for years. In addition, they have trouble finding young leaders who are willing to do what it takes—the long hours and dedication—to get the job done.

Older leaders want the next generations to:

- Acknowledge their work and contributions.
- Support their relevancy now, not just in the past.
- Recognize the legacy they are leaving.

When older leaders are apprehensive that their work and their lifetime contributions are being set aside, they find it difficult to support the newer generations. Aging in the United States is not an easy process, and for the generation that has claimed it will be forever young, the idea that what they have to contribute is outdated is almost inconceivable. Given the increase in U.S. life expectancy, it is no wonder that boomers are not ready to hand over their leadership. They see themselves continuing to be involved for years to come, even if they do not stay in their current jobs.

But even those who are ready to retire look to new leaders for acknowledgment. They are surprised when they are not tapped for information or ideas. In a meeting on legacy, baby boom leaders became teary when they thought about how much their work had meant to them.[19] They have a deep desire to know that what they have contributed will somehow live on. This is no surprise. No one wants to be irrelevant, set aside, or ignored.

Laying the Groundwork

The desire of older leaders for recognition of the hard work that has been done is not unreasonable. Nor is it out of bounds for younger generations to learn about both the successes and challenges of past social change work. Without blame or accusations, there is time to learn how to reach across generations to build an understanding of the different contributions each generation can make. In the next chapter, we look at what bonds us across generations and the different roles generations play as a way to prepare for moving ahead.

Notes

1. "Baby Boom." *Time*, February 9, 1948; "Babies Mean Business." *Newsweek*, August 9, 1948.
2. Lancaster, L. C., and Stillman, D. *When Generations Collide: Who They Are. Why They Clash. How to Solve the Generational Puzzle at Work*. New York: HarperCollins, 2002.
3. Gillon, S. *Boomer Nation: The Largest and Richest Generation Ever and How It Changed America*. New York: Free Press, 2004; Freedman, M. *Prime Time: How Baby Boomers Will Revolutionize Retirement and Transform America*. New York: PublicAffairs, 2004; Steinborn, L. *The Greater Generation: In Defense of the Baby Boomer Legacy*. New York: Thomas Dunne Books, 2006; Croker, R. *The Boomer Century, 1946–2046: How America's*

Most Influential Generation Changed Everything. New York: Springboard Press, 2007.

4. In this section, we discuss the baby boom population but include the late veterans of change who had many of the same experiences.

5. Lancaster, L., and Stillman, D. *When Generations Collide: Who They Are. Why They Clash. How to Solve the Generational Puzzle at Work.* New York: HarperCollins, 2002.

6. Coupland, D. *Generation X: Tales for an Accelerated Culture.* New York: St. Martin's Press, 1991.

7. Filipczak, B., Raines, C., and Zemke, R. *Generations at Work: Managing the Clash of Veterans, Boomers, Xers, and Nexters in Your Workplace.* New York: AMACOM, 2001; Halstead, T. "A Politics for Generation X." *The Atlantic Monthly,* August 1999; Hornblower, M. "Great Xpectations." *Time,* June 9, 1997; Tulgan, B. *Managing Generation X: How to Bring Out the Best in Young Talent.* New York: Norton and Company, 1996; Lancaster, L., and Stillman, D. *When Generations Collide: Who They Are. Why They Clash. How to Solve the Generational Puzzle at Work.* New York: HarperCollins, 2002.

8. Cryer, S. *The Nonprofit Career Guide: How to Land a Job That Makes a Difference.* St. Paul, Minn.: Fieldstone Alliance, 2008.

9. The Nonprofit Workforce Coalition has launched a comprehensive program to address this gap. See www.humanics.org/coalition.

10. For a more comprehensive discussion of staff entering social change work, see Chetkovich, C., and Kunreuther, F. *From the Ground Up: Grassroots Organizations Making Social Change.* Ithaca, N.Y.: Cornell University Press, 2006.

11. Mirabella, R., and Wish, N. "University-Based Educational Programs in the Management of Nonprofit Organizations: An Updated Census of U.S. Programs." *Public Performance and Management Review,* Sept. 2001, 25(1), 30–41.

12. This ambivalence is echoed in Cornelius, M., Corvington, P., and Ruesga, A. *Ready to Lead? Next Generation Leaders Speak Out*. Washington, D.C.: The Meyer Foundation, 2008.

13. Kunreuther, F. *Generational Change in Leadership: Implications for Social Change Organizations*. Cambridge, Mass.: Building Movement Project, 2002.

14. Collins, J. *Good to Great: Why Some Companies Make the Leap and Others Don't*. New York: HarperCollins, 2001; Gladwell, M. *The Tipping Point: How Little Things Can Make a Big Difference*. New York: Little, Brown, 2000.

15. Cornelius, M., Corvington, P., and Ruesga, A. *Ready to Lead? Next Generation Leaders Speak Out*. Washington, D.C.: The Meyer Foundation, 2008.

16. Solomon, J., and Sandahl, Y. *Out and Back: A National Survey of Next-Generation Potential Leaders in the Nonprofit Sector*. Washington, D.C.: Young Nonprofit Professionals Network, 2007. The most common reasons for leaving were burnout, low compensation, lack of career advancement, and job-related stress.

17. Kunreuther, F., Blain, L., and Fellner, K. *Generational Leadership Listening Sessions*. New York: Building Movement Project, 2004; *Life's Work: Generational Attitudes Toward Work and Life Integration*. Cambridge, Mass.: The Radcliffe Public Policy Center with Harris Interactive, 2000.

18. "Americans Work Longest Hours Among Industrialized Countries." *ILO News*. www.hartford-hwp.com/archives/26/077.html (September 6, 1999); Anderson, P. "Study: U.S. Employees Put in Most Hours." *CNN Career*. http://archives.cnn.com/2001/CAREER/trends/08/30/ilo.study/ (August 31, 2001).

19. "What Remains—A Consultative Session on Legacy." Meeting at Annie E. Casey Foundation, June 4–15, 2007, Baltimore, Md.

3

ROLES AND VALUES

Laying the Groundwork

None of us wants to be seen as too inexperienced, irrelevant, or obsolete, no matter what our age. In this chapter we take a step back to look at two frameworks that help us understand the larger context in which leaders in the social sector operate. The roles framework presents how different generations are working on different tasks in their life cycle, which influences how they approach leadership and how they relate to other generations. The second framework looks at values and explores how values can build bonds between generations in order to work toward a common vision.

Different Generations, Different Roles

Differences in how generations approach leadership are based not only on each cohort's experiences but also on their stage of life. In this section, we outline the nonprofit leadership roles and the work that needs to be accomplished based on the position in the life cycle. We then look at the ways generations can support each other. How we view ourselves and the world changes as we age and approach different developmental tasks, with each change affecting work, family life, and the general sense of what is needed for a feeling of well-being.[1] Each generation's leadership role in social sector work reflects its stage of life and the unique circumstances of the age cohort. Table 3.1 outlines some of the important leadership tasks of the four generations in the workplace: the millennium generation, Generation X, baby boomers, and veterans of change.

Table 3.1.   Different Generations, Different Tasks

Millennials: **Development**	• Focus on how to apply learning and ideas to work setting. • Acquire skills in work. • Practice critical analysis of the world as it is versus what it claims to be. • Generate ideas of different approaches to the work. • Extend view of work and possible roles. • Learn assumptions underlying current social change work. • Develop an identity with communities of choice. • Move quickly among tasks.
Generation X: **Establishment**	• Move from focus on own identity to the field. • Gain mastery in content areas. • Expand assumptions about making change. • Solidify and extend relationships. • Stretch to incorporate new skills and deepen understanding of work. • Find or create opportunities to implement ideas. • Broaden experience in directing others. • Continue learning from own and others' experiences.
Baby Boomers: **Assessment**	• Take stock of areas of influence and power. • Use influence, experience, and relationships to make change. • Unite with others for power. • Teach and draw out new partners in order to have a larger impact. • Offer to bridge new relationships to promote change. • Reflect on learning, and consolidate to pass on to others. • Promote promising leadership to support the next phase of work. • Help increase influence on new leaders. • Begin to think of legacy.

Veterans *of Change:* **Contribution**	• Complete plan to leave the organization, and consider other roles to make a contribution.
	• Assess legacy; release power and control.
	• Support leaders currently in power by using contacts and relationships.
	• Find ways to learn from younger leadership and offer them ideas, experience, and expertise.
	• Take note of how work has changed over time.
	• Reflect on success, and analyze failures.
	• Record information about experiences.

The skills and developmental tasks identified in Table 3.1 summarize each generation's primary identification now (development, establishment, assessment, contribution). The millennial generation, just entering the workforce, is in the developmental stage; they are running businesses and heading new social ventures. This generation, recognized for idealism and technological savvy, will bring new expertise to the older groups while considering their own identity. Millennials are developing critical thinking skills, generating ideas about how change can be made, and thinking about their future roles.

Generation Xers, with significant experience under their belt, are working to establish their positions as leaders. They are expanding their work and networks, looking to create opportunities where they can do social change work and flexing their muscle. Still in a learning mode, they are wrestling with issues related to management and leadership. This is a time when they will deepen their understanding of how to do their work and have an impact on their field.

Boomers are in power and are using their influence to partner with others in their cohort to make change. They have consolidated their authority and are enjoying their continued leadership roles. At the same time, they are assessing how their work can make a lasting impact and thinking about the legacy they will leave. They need to identify new leadership and start to pass on skills and relationships that will help those coming up behind them build the power they need to succeed.

Veterans of change have left or are in the process of leaving their jobs. They are seeking ways to scale back while still using their former sway to make contributions to social change. They are moving from a position of power to a period where they will have time to consider their successes and failures and pass on their observations to younger generations. As they relinquish control, they will have time to listen to and encourage newer generations, assuming they are willing and able to bridge the generation divide.

Support for Leadership Across Generations

Different generations of nonprofit leadership also have specific roles to play in relation to other generations. Table 3.2 outlines the ways that each generation reacts to the others and the support and challenges they can offer. Table 3.3 identifies how generations can discourage one another, that is, what

Table 3.2.   What We Do for Other Generations

Millennials: **Learn and Confront**	• Learn from Gen X and baby boomers both the content of the work and the way it is currently done.
	• Confront older generations, especially Gen X and baby boomers, by raising new ways to do the work.
	• Make mistakes; learn from experience.
	• Respect contributions of older generations, especially boomers and veterans of change.
	• Connect with and push against Generation X.
Generation X: **Support and Push**	• Support the development of millennials, and learn from their ideas.
	• Expect pressure from millennials to institute new ways to do the work.
	• Push up against baby boomers with both content knowledge and experience from a decade in the field.

- Partner with baby boomers to move work ahead and make needed changes.
- Bridge millennium and boomer generations.
- Learn from veterans of change.

Baby Boomers: **Partner and Challenge**	• Partner with Generation X, bringing them into leadership, including giving them significant responsibility and authority. • Challenge and push Gen X to build leadership skills. • Encourage millennials through acknowledgment and attention. • Acknowledge the work of veterans of change generation and assure them their legacy will be carried on. • Recognize that social change does not start and end with their generation.
Veterans of Change: **Mentor and Remind**	• Mentor Generation X and millennials by listening to their grievances and supporting their desire to make change. • Remind baby boomers that though they are now in power, they should start to prepare the next generation of leadership. • Offer honest assessments of recent history, and remind others of values and elements of change. • Listen and reminisce when asked.

Table 3.3.   How We Can Discourage Other Generations

Millennials	• Ignore previous generations and lose ground by not learning from the past.
Generation X	• Remain alienated from other generations and opt out of leadership.
Baby Boomers	• Refuse to plan for or support new leadership and try to stay in power.
Veterans of Change	• Dismiss younger generations, become disaffected, neglect to pass on important information, and opt out.

each generation could do that would be harmful to generating new leadership or learning from the past in social change nonprofits.

It makes sense that veterans of change would see their role as mentoring and reminding those who are younger of what came before them. They can support new generations by listening and offering encouragement and conveying a long-term view of change. As the oldest generation in the workplace, they remind baby boomers to use their power and influence well and to prepare for their future. If they choose, they can offer narratives that provide important information for the next generations. However, older leaders also can disappear, literally or figuratively, leaving younger generations without the support and information they could use to ease their work moving forward.

Baby boomers, at the height of their power, are at a point where they can pause to give honor and tribute to this older generation and recognize that social change did not start (and end) with them. Boomers need to focus on how they partner with and challenge Generation X, viewing them as colleagues and encouraging them not to be complacent about their role or ideas. They also can build relationships with millennials, offering them new opportunities that will stretch them to learn within and outside their work. Boomers can discourage younger generations by keeping control rather than passing it on in a coherent and thoughtful manner, thus thwarting new leadership and stagnating movement for change.

Generation X is in the squeeze between the boomers and millennials. They will both support millennials and push baby boomers. They are looking for a way to partner with and learn from the boomers at the same time they will press them on accepting new ideas. As the bridge generation, Xers need to encourage the millennials, who are already nipping at their heels. Following the dominance of baby boomer leaders, Generation X might also become alienated from other generations, keeping younger leaders at bay and resenting the lengthening stay and power of the boomers.

As the youngest cohort, the millennium generation should expect support from baby boomers and Generation X even though they will confront these older cohorts about their views and assumptions. They are quick to learn from other generations, even those they rebel against. This challenge, to learn and confront, is important: it keeps ideas for social change current and helps to integrate the freshness brought in by a new generation. Millennials could make the mistake of assuming that in such a fast-paced world, they can ignore the advice and work of those who precede them, thus losing ground in the fight for change.

These roles are not fixed, but they provide a way to understand how each generation is needed to build and solidify ongoing leadership and press social sector work forward. The ability to recognize different generations' leadership trajectory provides a guide for how to view differences. If baby boomers are not thinking about training new leaders or bringing Generation X leaders in as colleagues, they slow the progress of their organizations and the broader work for social change. If Generation X is not finding or creating new opportunities for themselves, they become bitter and lose sight of the contributions they are already making and the ones they will make in the future. Patronizing millennials will result in a generation that has new ideas and methods of communicating but will be moving forward without a sense of history, which will lessen their impact. Learning how to work together across the generational divides can produce something powerful that paves the road toward our vision of the future.

Exercise 3.1 "What Do They Think of Me?" surfaces some of the real and perceived differences among the generations in a fun and interactive way. Each age cohort is asked to come up with what they believe the other generations say or think about them.

Exercise 3.1
What Do They Think of Me?

This exercise should be used with a mixed-age group; a facilitator is needed to give instructions and facilitate the debriefing process.

Step 1

- Ask people to form small groups based on their age cohorts. The easiest way to do this is for the facilitator to share the years that constitute different generations and ask participants to group themselves by their generational designations: millennials (born after 1980), Generation X (born 1965 to 1980), baby boomers (born 1946 to 1964), and veterans for change (born before 1946). In some cases, depending on the number of people in each group, the facilitator may combine groups, such as baby boomers and veterans of change or separate groups into older and younger baby boomers.

- Each group should get a marker and flip chart. On the flip chart, make one column for each generation that is not the group's own. For example, millennials would make a column for Generation X, boomers, and veterans of change.

Step 2

- Have each group write on the flip chart under the appropriate column what they believe the other generations think of them. For example, Generation X participants might say baby boomers find them too entitled and millennials find them too conservative.

- Give each group about five minutes on each of the other generations. Remember that this should be a fun and spontaneous activity; encourage groups to quickly fill out each column on the flip chart.

Step 3

- When the groups have completed their lists, have the full group stand around each flip chart while the cohort that filled out the chart presents the lists.

- After each group presents, the facilitator asks the presenting cohort about their process:
  - Did the members of the group disagree?
  - If so on what issues? Were there things you decided not to put on the chart? What were they, and why did you make that decision?
- The facilitator asks each of the other age groups that are not presenting the following questions:
  - What do they think of what was said about their generation?
  - Does it ring true? Why or why not?

Step 4

After all the age groups have presented, have the large group discuss what they have learned through this exercise. The facilitator should guide the group discussion using these questions:

- What are the similarities and differences in each generation's report?
- Why do you think these similarities and differences exist?
- What surprised you about these responses?
- What insights have you gained about how to have a better understanding of each generation based on this exercise and discussion?

The facilitator should make sure that the group discusses how we all carry stereotypes about our own generation and about others. Stereotypes have kernels of truth, but they can also confine us from building connections across generations.

Using the Roles Frame

Understanding the roles different people play helps to see each generation's actions and reactions within a context. It also is a starting point for discussions about similarities and differences between different age cohorts. We suggest keeping this frame in mind as a way to remember that roles and positions are not stagnant and that the process of generation change is not only about the content of the work but also about the shifts that generations constantly navigate over their lifetime.

What Bonds Us Across Generations: The Role of Values

Those working for social change have more in common than they acknowledge.[2] Among social change leaders, there are similarities in their commitment to work and their long-term goals. One way to understand these commonalities among different generations is through a values frame.

Although the world is changing at a rapid pace, generational shifts are gradual, taking place over many years and in many different ways. One thing that will unite different age cohorts is their common beliefs and values. Values are "principles or standards of behavior."[3] They are deeply felt and difficult to articulate. Yet it is crucial to include them when we think about leadership, especially in the mission-driven work of the nonprofit sector, where values are the foundation of social change vision. For example, one value for progressive social change might be the belief that there should be equal treatment and equity across race, class, gender and gender identity, religion, sexual orientation, caste, and other boundaries. Another might be the way we behave with one another, such as showing respect and generosity. How values are enacted may differ across many different traditions, including generations.

In this section, we highlight three important elements of values: vision, trust, and awareness (see Figure 3.1). These three concepts are the foundation that guides the work of social sector organizations and of progressive movements. They are mutually

Figure 3.1.   Values Frame

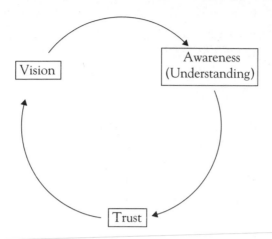

reinforcing to keep us on track when we are lost in our day-to-day work.

Values articulate aspirations; they sustain us through disagreements, misunderstandings, and differences. Vision, awareness, and trust are activities that support values and help them grow.

Vision

Vision is a good place to start a discussion of values. All social change organizations have a vision, either explicit or assumed. The vision is the world that the organization wants to create; it therefore represents the spirit of the work. The vision helps to connect groups with their colleagues and keep them moving together to build a better world. In some organizations, staff, board, constituents, members, and volunteers discuss how they see the long-term future and develop a vision statement. The vision is the organizational glue that reminds everyone not to lose sight of the larger purpose, even in the face of opposition. The vision helps those working for social change remember they are all moving in the same direction even when they may not agree on the strategies and actions for how to get there.

Sample Mission and Vision Statements

MISSION

Enlacé Comunitario's mission is to work with Latino immigrants to eliminate domestic violence and strengthen their community.

VISION

We envision a city, state, and nation where immigrants can become a collective, conscious, free, and powerful force dedicated to the eradication of violence and the elimination of barriers to success.

Trust

Social change takes both a vision about the world that can be shared and the conviction that, together and over time, it is possible to reach the vision. The key to doing this is trust. Trust, defined as "the firm belief in the reliability, truth, ability, or strength of someone," is the most underestimated building block in the cycle of change.[4]

To develop trust, we need to create opportunities to share experiences, talk about our own history and perspectives, and find ways to learn from one another. Since trust is built over time, it is natural to trust those with whom you have a long history. It takes conscious effort to create trust across generations that might have fewer naturally shared experiences.

Leadership Change and the Role of Trust

Lack of trust can result in unintended consequences. Consider the experience of a veteran of change founder from a key social change organization who hired a vibrant group of young staffers in anticipation of his own transition. He began planning with the board chair a process for changing roles. But the new staffers, who loved the organization and had great respect for the founder, felt left

out of these conversations, and as time progressed they
began to talk about leaving. In this case, there was a shared
vision, but the trust between the founder and board chair,
on the one hand, and the new staff, on the other, had not
been sufficiently established. The founder assumed it was
his responsibility to make the plan. The new staff felt they
had little voice in planning for the future of the organization.
Fortunately, some younger board members saw what was
happening and suggested that the board and staff meet
with a facilitator to build deeper relationships and a better
understanding of how different people in the organization
viewed the leadership shifts. Rebuilding the trust led to the
adoption of a transition plan that took into account the
needs of both generations, was supported by the board, and
built on the strong reputation of the organization.

Trust is an important foundation to support each other despite the inevitable disagreements that occur among generations. In the spirit of generous leadership, trust is something that can be offered by older generations to newer ones, rather than something that is withheld until younger ones prove they are worthy. Exercises 3.2 to 3.5 on pages 68–71 offer a series of reflective practices to help organizational leaders think about how to build trust with their staff and board members. They can be done separately, but they are most useful together as one builds on the other.

Awareness

Generational awareness, which may also be referred to as consciousness or understanding, is the third element in the values frame. Awareness helps to bridge generational differences through developing a shared understanding about the underlying structures that need to change in order to reach the organization's vision.

Within generations, we often have an unspoken understanding or analysis of how things operate. There are common markers that are used as reference points or shortcuts in the ways an age cohort describes what needs to be done. But what seems obvious within a generation can be a mystery to those outside it. Our values may be the same, but each generation has its own developmental landmarks, skills, abilities, and

Exercise 3.2
Understanding Trust

Step 1

Drawing from your work and life experience, think of a few people whom you trust and how you have come to trust them. Write down specific acts or experiences that helped you to trust them.

Whom I Trust	How I Got to Know This Person	Key Factors, Acts, and Communications That Were Critical in Building Trust with This Person

Step 2

Review your responses:

- What are important things that help you trust other people?
- How can others know this about you so they can build trust with you?

Exercise 3.3
Building Trust in the Workplace

Step 1

While building trust among all staff members is important, there are also some key people in the organization whose trust in you is particularly helpful. List their names on the top row of the table, and answer the questions on the left-hand column for each person.

	Name	*Name*	*Name*	*Name*
Person whose trust is important to me				
Why is this person's trust important to me?				
How did I or can I gain this person's trust?				
What specific acts, communications, or something else helped or will help to build trust?				
How do I or will I know that this person trusts me?				

Step 2

Debrief using these questions:

- Remember that trust building takes both intention and time. What are some first steps you will take to build trust with these people?

- Looking at your responses, are there things that you are not sure of? What can you do to get the information you need?

Exercise 3.4
Practicing Trust-Building Culture in the Workplace

These questions can be used at a staff meeting or retreat to talk about how to take steps to create a culture of trust building in the organization.

Step 1

Bring the group into a large circle. Go around the circle, asking each person to share one response to the question, "What are some words and actions that help to foster trust among staff?" You may go around one more time to generate more ideas. List the responses on a flip chart.

Step 2

Repeat Step 1 with this question: "What are some words and actions that can lead to lack of trust?"

Step 3

Review the responses to both questions with the group. Break the full group into small groups and discuss these questions:

- What do we do well in our organization to foster trust?
- What can we improve to create a more trust-building culture?

Step 4

Bring the full group back into the circle to report. Pay attention to both broad themes and specific requests for actions. Based on the responses, have a discussion on some things that everyone is willing to do in the next month to help create a stronger trust-building culture in the organization. These can be a collective commitment as well as an individual commitment.

Exercise 3.5
Building Trust with the Board

Trust between the board and the executive director is important in building a healthy organization and preparing the organization for any change in leadership in the future. This exercise is a way to help executive directors think more concretely about how to build trust with board leadership. This exercise can also be done with leadership teams.

Step 1

Complete the table for each board officer or other volunteer leader.

Board member name and title			
Board member's primary interests/roles on the board and in the organization			
What the member has said or done to indicate trust in you or your leadership			
What the member has said or done to indicate mistrust of you or your leadership			
What steps you can take to build trust with the person			

Step 2

Review your responses:

- How can you communicate to your board members that you want to build more trust with them?

- Who else can support you in developing a board that has a high level of trust in the executive director?

strategies. There is a certain recognition we have with our own age group, ethnicity, region, and other characteristics that binds us together. And there are often limits to how well we see things from another's point of view.

Awareness is a process that helps us understand not only what is evident to our age group but also see how others analyze issues or problems. In social change, awareness or consciousness is a way to see how inequality, inequity, and lack of sustainability persist in spite of changes on the surface. It is a way to unveil what would otherwise be invisible, such as how tax cuts radically alter our country's investment in public schools, health care, and libraries while dramatically increasing the number of billionaires in the United States or the way pollutants are dumped in low-income communities, contaminating vital resources.

The importance of awareness is political but also personal. The value of awareness keeps us looking deeper to find real causes and real connections in our work so we can have a common understanding.

The values frame—understanding the role of vision, trust, and awareness—is one way to see the continuity between generations. We need to consciously pass on the knowledge and experience of older generations and learn about the current realities and views of the future from those who are younger.

Working effectively across generations in the social sector includes understanding the roles we have as we move through the life cycle and having structured and institutionalized methods to learn and listen to one another on issues such as building power, relationships, and leadership. In Chapter Six we offer some structured ideas for how such learning can happen. First, however, we look at how older and younger leaders are planning for their future.

Help in Talking About Values

If you decide to talk about values in your organization, coalition, or other group, remember to involve everyone. Here are some approaches to use:

- Surface differences. *Talking about values means that differences will be opened up and discussed. This is often the hardest part of our work: handling differences in a productive and respectful way. It takes leadership to help people share their beliefs including a generosity of spirit so we can find our common ground.*

- Discover what we share. *We often hear people talk about the disintegration of values, the lack of values, or differences in values. Leadership for social change means recognizing and amplifying shared values.*

- Make it possible. *We have often seen leaders use values as a weapon to hurt others, yet values can bring us together and nurture us. Leadership for social change challenges people to use values to express what is possible rather than what is wrong.*

Notes

1. Erikson, E. H. *Identity and the Life Cycle*. New York: W. W. Norton, 1980.
2. Gillon, S. *Boomer Nation: The Largest and Richest Generation Ever and How It Changed America*. New York: Free Press, 2004.
3. "Value." *Oxford English Dictionary*. Retrieved May 23, 2008, www.askoxford.com/concise_oed/value.
4. "Trust." *Oxford English Dictionary*. Retrieved May 23, 2008, www.askoxford.com/concise_oed/trust.

Part Two

SHIFTS HAPPEN: MOVING FORWARD

4

THE BOOMERS ARE LEAVING?

I want to work in a place that is not so fraught
with responsibility. How little can I work and still
maintain the life I want . . . something meaningful?

I think people are not thinking about getting old.
Maybe because people are living longer and are
active so people don't think about it. I am thinking
about it in the political context of movement
building, because this movement needs so many
leaders. . . . We want to have a constructive role in
the movement. What should our relationship be
with people who take over?

The time to prepare for the coming decades is now. In this
and the next chapter, we discuss what older and younger generations of social change leaders are looking forward to as they
think ahead. Boomers and veterans of change must figure out
their contributions either in their last years as leaders or when
they leave their positions. Younger generations are confronting
decisions about where they see themselves in the future—in the
social sector or outside—and the role they will play.

This chapter is about older leaders. We have already challenged the commonly held assumption that the nonprofit sector is in a crisis because of the imminent exodus of the baby
boom generation. Although their dominant role in the sector's
top positions has many buzzing about a future without them,
their longevity, age span, and cohort size make it likely that
their departure will take place gradually over the next decades.

This provides the sector with a transition period and the space to consider new ways to think about retirement, organizational structure, and leadership positions.

Retirement or Retrenchment?

Baby boomers are once again breaking new ground. They are a generation that will redefine aging not only because of their lust for life but because of the facts. Longevity has been increasing in the United States for decades. Technological and scientific advancements make perpetual youth, through medical intervention, lifestyle adjustment, and environmental change, seem within reach. When Social Security benefits began in the 1930s, it was assumed that the first recipients, at age sixty-two, would live another decade.[1] Now people routinely live well into their nineties, and Hallmark touts the number of people who buy Happy Hundredth Birthday cards. So when boomers say that seventy is the new fifty, they are not simply talking about their aspirations.

In our discussions with baby-boom-age nonprofit leaders, many are thoughtful about the future—for both themselves and their organizations. They are aware of the challenges ahead and eager to discuss their changing role over the next decades. Three themes dominate: (1) whether boomers will be able to retire, (2) what their involvement in change work will be, and (3) how and when to exit in a productive manner. In these conversations, it particularly struck us that many boomer leaders are looking to the future with anxiety.

Challenges in Moving Forward

It used to be that when you turned sixty, you were heading into what was referred to as the golden years. It was a time of leisure, when you were freed from the drudgery of your job and could do the things you had no time for while you worked and raised a family. But times have changed.

As the life span has been extended, so has the need to save money to be able to enjoy the golden years. Retirement age for many has become a moving target, a calculation that seems increasingly complicated with volatile financial markets and threatened public benefits. In addition, baby boomers are less interested in the traditional idea of retirement. They want to keep doing, making a contribution, and having a role. This is especially true for those in nonprofits, where work coincides with deeply held values of service and change. When will boomer leaders in the social sector leave their jobs? No one knows, but we do know that several issues will influence their decision.

Money Matters

Information on the financial situation for aging boomers who work in nonprofits is sorely lacking. There is little information about their savings, retirement funds, or pension benefits or about whether they are the primary source of income in their families. As a generation, baby boomers are often portrayed as having failed to make financial plans for the future. And there is the anticipation that some will be affluent based on the expected massive transfer of wealth from their more frugal parents.

Whatever the situation may be, many aging nonprofit leaders are worried about their financial security. Those in top positions may make larger salaries than their staffers, but in small and midsized organizations, that still might not be enough to leave even a relatively high-paying job at age sixty-five. We found that executives who made well into six figures, as well as those who never reached an annual salary of fifty thousand dollars, expressed similar concerns about their financial future. Salary was not the only issue. Until they are eligible for government health benefits, and even after, boomers are unwilling to risk giving up even meager health insurance. Moreover, there is apprehension about the viability of government-funded programs such as Medicare and Social Security.

Money looms large for baby boomer leaders for other reasons too. Boomers' living parents are now in decline, and the cost of care may add to the budget or money boomers expected to inherit will be used up. In addition, the baby boom cohort tended to have their children later than those in earlier generations, and many are either still supporting them at home, anticipating college tuition, or helping them out once they are grown but not yet independent. Fluctuations in financial markets make savings more tenuous, and even the increased value of their homes may be in jeopardy as the bubble bursts.

Executives who want to step back from a top leadership position but still need a salary feel particularly vulnerable. Where to go next is often unclear, and despite the boomers' youthfulness, they are growing older. There is concern about ageism, especially for older women, and fears that boomers will be threatening to existing directors if they take a less prestigious role. AARP's Web site gives interview tips to mature job seekers reminding them to "talk only about your past experiences that are related to the job you're applying for" and "avoid telling the [younger] employer what they could do better or are doing wrong."

One boomer left a coveted leadership job when she became ill. In her mid-fifties and on the market, she began to lose confidence that her talents would be recognized by potential employers who might label her as too old or too experienced for a less stressful situation. As her severance pay began to run out, she decided to accept a position that was far beneath her skill level. A year later, she reentered the job market and found a higher-level spot in her old field, but the situation is not secure, and she worries about what she will do if the funding runs out.

Finally, retirement for the boomer generation might just cost more than they originally planned. With the cost of living accelerating and the dollar weakening, it is not clear what it will take to maintain a comfortable lifestyle. This can affect those with few resources and others as well. After all, social sector leaders who leave their positions are unlikely to want to sit at home. Many have been waiting for the time when they will be able to travel, spend time with their family and friends, and feel unencumbered in ways that have a price tag. So with decades ahead of them, when do they decide to leave or cut down on the job—and the income?

Money does matter, and many boomer leaders and staff members in the social sector have a long way to go before they are financially secure enough to leave behind paid work.

Where to Go?

Even leaders who could retire may decide not to do so, because money is not the only thing that matters to boomer leaders. They have often spent decades building organizations and have enormous pride in and attachment to their work. Their identity, as we have noted, is tied to the position and organization. One executive director asked, "What does my business card say if I leave my job?"

In truth, unless there is something else they want to do, why would boomers who are still relatively young give up the satisfaction and recognition they receive from their work? For many, time has passed quickly, and they have a finite period left to accomplish the things they want for their organizations and make a significant impact in the field. One boomer leader expressed shock when he realized he had been at the same job for almost twenty years. In his mid-fifties, he now assumes he will stay at least another decade before retiring. The organization has an excellent reputation and many successes, and he has good relations with the board of directors and staff members. Fundraising, though always a challenge, is at this point routine. He is well established in the community and has energy and passion for the work—why would he look for a new position where he would have to start over?

When asked about their future plans, many boomer leaders were clearly taken off guard. One remarked,

I don't know. I'll just keep doing what I've been doing. I don't have any plans. You know it remains interesting, because we're always doing new things. . . . How long would I continue to do this? I don't know what else I would do if I didn't do something like this.

Another had thought about his future but was both clear and humorous about his tenure in the job:

To be honest, I have no idea. I'll probably keep going, doing this stuff, until I drop dead. In fact, I'll probably drop dead right in this chair, like I always tell my staff. One day somebody's going to come in in the morning, and I'm going to be dead. So that's as much as I can tell you about that.

Leaving top positions means coping with the loss of status as well. It is often stunning to long-term leaders how quickly they can be forgotten by their organizations and in the field. Leaving a position of high visibility and authority can be daunting. After so many years, there is often little recognition of a leader who has dedicated a lifetime to change work once they have left the job.

How to Decide?

As with any other major life transition, older leaders usually need an extended period of consideration and consultation before deciding to leave their jobs. Given the size of the boomer generation, we would expect that these conversations would be common, even supported, in the social sector. Yet boomer executive directors and CEOs reported that it was difficult to find places where they could openly and safely consider their next steps. Outside of their family and closest friends, they fear that even a preliminary exploration of how long they might remain in their position could have dire consequences.

For example, confiding in boards of directors poses a challenge even for long-term directors. Most leaders are the linchpin between the organization and the board of directors. They fear the board will take a conversation about future plans as a signal to convince the current director to stay or, worse, a green light to start recruiting new leadership. Board members may also be financial supporters of the organization. That leads to a concern about the reaction of high-end donors, program officers, or public grants administrators if they find out that a trusted leader is thinking about next steps. And staffers, often the people closest to the director, are the most vulnerable when there is an executive change. Leaders are rightly concerned that open discussion can lead to a sense of instability within the organization.

Many do not even trust their colleagues when it comes to talking seriously about next steps. "I talk to friends but not colleagues because it doesn't feel safe," explained one boomer. "But I constantly talk about it with friends. When I stop doing this work, I know I can't stop working. But what will I do? I consider it the next phase . . . because I don't have personal wealth that will allow me not to work. But it looks different from a nine-to-seven, seven-day-a-week job."

Yet colleagues are often the best advisers. In one city, we held a discussion group with baby boom and Generation X leaders that drove home how lonely planning their next steps can be for older generations. We divided into small groups by age. The boomer-age leaders veered off from the assigned topic to share how they were thinking about the future. One was making plans to leave but worried about finding a suitable replacement. Another ran a small organization she had created many years ago and wondered whether the organization could survive if she cut back her hours. Others talked about the high cost of living, supporting their children through college, and other similar matters. When it was time to reconvene, it was hard to stop the flood of conversation. Later, one of the participants told us how rare it is that older organizational leaders come together to discuss their future.

The desire to talk is often intertwined with leaders' worries about how the organization will fare without them. Everyone has a nightmare story of an organization failing after the exit of a long-term director or founder. One boomer leader, who saw the nonprofit she built disintegrate after her departure, talked about the "shock when your organization falls apart." Her decision to help save the group meant she had to consider what role she would play: "Rebuilding, renegotiating your relationship to it. . . . How do you . . . see what you can let go of?"

Directors also worry about how their organizations will change once they leave. After years of dedication, it can be painful to find that one's replacement is taking the group in a new direction or shifting priorities. One founder carefully planned her departure with her board of directors, who stressed the need to fill the position with someone who could maintain the values and spirit of the organization. But two executive directors later, the group is struggling. It turned out that even someone with the right principles was not always prepared for the management and fundraising that was necessary for survival.

Of course, many organizations make successful executive transitions, but these uncertainties can deter ambivalent leaders from opening up a conversation about what is next. Nevertheless we worry that if executive directors do not discuss their own future with board and staff members, their organizations will suffer. As directors age, succession becomes the elephant in the room. Everyone wonders what will happen, but no one wants to raise the question. Nevertheless, conversations about an older leader's plans that are undertaken with careful consideration can make room for other important discussions, such as internal leadership development, organizational health, and future directions.

Planning for Transition

Although each boomer leader and organization will have a unique experience of change, there are useful frames that can help groups prepare. Organizational expert William Bridges, who has written extensively on transitions, points out that change and transition are different: change is situational, and transition is psychological.[2] Transition requires recognizing the ending, mourning the loss, and then letting go. Even when a leader is ready to move on and an organization is well prepared for a new director, it is important to recognize the need to let go of the old reality and prepare for a new beginning. Leadership transitions on boards of directors and in key staff positions also affect the organization. Yet the departure of the top leader is often the most difficult to fully address.

In Exercise 4.1, we apply Bridges's concepts to help older leaders start to think about their transitions. The transitions concept can be used with any change, but it is particularly helpful in preparing individuals and organizations for the emotional feelings that accompany leadership shifts rather than simply focusing on the mechanics.

Exercise 4.1
Preparing for Transitions

Transition has three phases: coming to an end, a period of mourning the loss (sometimes mixed with feelings of excitement), and the time to let go fully. In this exercise, we ask you to look back to a time in your life when you went through a major life and work transition. This can be done individually or with a group if the group went through a common experience of transition together. Encouraging other organizational leaders, such as secondary leaders and board members, to participate in this exercise will build a deeper understanding and empathy for the transition process.

Step 1

First think about one transition you went through in the past. It can be work related, such as taking a new position, or something in your personal life. Recall the highlights of that event, and jot them down on paper to help you remember the emotions you experienced connected to that event.

(continued)

Exercise 4.1
Preparing for Transitions (*continued*)

Step 2

Answer the questions that follow. Give specific examples because these will be helpful in identifying future steps:

- How did you know that the previous phase ended? What things occurred?

- What emotions did you experience? What helped you move through that process? How long did it take?

- What helped you let go of the previous phase? What happened when you let go?

Step 3

Review your responses to the questions in step 2, and reflect on the following:

- What do these responses tell you about how you approach major transitions in your work and the rest of you life?

- Are there things you want to build on or do differently in your future transitions?

- What can make your next transition a more positive experience?

Step 4

Based on the responses to the next two questions, decide what concrete steps you can begin to take.

- What can you do now to approach your transition?

- What can you ask other staff and board members in the organization to do now to help prepare for a healthy leadership transition?

Thinking about and preparing for transition may seem obvious, but in the high-activity, often-emergency-filled work of many nonprofits, where meeting mission and raising funds take priority, it is easy to ignore basic planning for change. In addition, for long-time leaders, it is an emotion-filled process, one that both leaders and organizations may want to avoid. Finally, there is the impact on organizations, which often hold the memory and the practices of leaders long after their departure. Awareness of the process can make a significant difference in letting go of what has been and opening up to what is to come.

Looking Ahead

Older leaders for the most part are confident that they will know when it is time to depart. But as we have seen, making this decision can be complicated by a leader's personal situation and the needs of the organization. Of course, the decision of older leaders to remain in their jobs or to leave is not theirs alone. They are responsible to the board of directors and the organization as a whole. Staying in the position should be based on their continued energy and commitment, ability to perform, and leadership qualities.

In this section we discuss the options older leaders are considering. Those who will remain for many years to come face the challenge of how they can be most effective over time and of the ways they will keep the organization energized and forward looking rather than resting on its past. Boomers preparing for their exit from their organization, leadership positions, or full-time work need to consider the transition they plan to make. Although there is no perfect way to stay or to go, there is the ability to be intentional and to take into consideration the impact on the individuals involved and the organization as a whole.

Staying in the Organization

Baby boomers who plan to continue to work in the sector's leadership roles will face the daily challenges that they have coped with for years. But they also have additional responsibilities. As they age, they need to ensure their organizations are relevant now and will continue to thrive once they leave. There are several issues in particular that we suggest they address: expanding and deepening the organization's secondary leadership, thinking about what the organization will need to survive, and considering other roles within the organization.

Leadership Development. One of the concerns we hear throughout the sector is that too little attention has been paid to the leadership development of young leaders. There is no better place to begin to address that problem than in organizations. Older leaders who plan to stay in their position for the coming years can play a significant role in this process to benefit not only their own work but the entire field. For older leaders, this means consciously thinking about how they transfer their knowledge to new generations and creating opportunities for younger staff to take on more responsibility and authority. Staff members, in turn, need to learn to rely on their own decision-making ability rather than look to the leader for constant affirmation.

The advantages of developing a deep and younger leadership bench even in small organizations are often overlooked. First and foremost, harried executive directors will have other leaders in the organization they can depend on to handle some of the work, such as program development, fundraising, supervising staff, or financial oversight. We know that many top leaders feel burdened by the multiple tasks and expectations of the job. Leadership development and allowing others in the organization to make decisions is one step in alleviating the problem.

Second, leadership development keeps an organization fresh by bringing in new and younger staffers with ideas and perceptions that may differ from those of the current leadership. The wisdom that comes from being on the job for many years is enhanced by amplifying the voices of others who bring additional perspectives.

Third, even if younger leaders leave the organization, the investment in their development creates a feeling of goodwill and connection that both builds the field and creates new opportunities for future collaborations. Leaders and organizations benefit when former staffers take on other leadership roles while maintaining good ties and high esteem for the group that invested in them. And it is easier to attract replacements when an organization has a reputation for building and supporting new leaders.

Finally, expanding the number of newer leaders can be a tremendous asset when a leadership change does take place. Staffers in the organization are prepared, and the organization believes it can survive beyond the current leader's tenure. In addition, one or more of the staffers may be ready to fill the position when the older leader does exit.

Organizational Structure. Young Shin, founding director of Asian Immigrant Women Advocates (AIWA), is used to working long hours. Recently she has decided to make some concrete changes in her work schedule with an eye toward the future:

> For the last two, three years, I've been really conscious about not doing more than full-time work. Because that's one of the things when the founder leaves, there are lots of problems because people forget that founders have been working around the clock. When this person leaves, it becomes a two- or three-person job. So I've been making some changes. And I've been trying to balance how much time I spend at work.

Young is one of many older leaders who is intentionally thinking while she is in the job about the organization's future without her. Knowing that the group's success depends in part on her long hours, she is making important adjustments now that will strengthen AIWA in the future.

For some boomer leaders, shedding certain job responsibilities is another way to prepare the organization for the eventual departure of a long-time director who is used to doing everything. One baby boom–age leader laid out his strategy: "So the major thing that we're trying to do now is we're trying to hire a COO, a chief operating officer—someone to take on my administrative tasks, although they're never all going to go. But I'm trying to get as many of the fundraising, financial oversight, evaluation, administration, administration, administration away from me."

This may sound like an ideal option for directors who want to have a manageable and more enjoyable workload and to start to pass on some of the important leadership responsibilities. Long-term leaders think about giving over areas that they find least gratifying to concentrate on the pieces they like best, including networking and program work. However, shifting job responsibilities in this way can have unintended consequences. On the one hand, it can distribute power within the organization rather than keeping it concentrated in one person. On the other hand, leaders may let go of what they like least without sharing decision making in areas such as vision, mission, and outcomes. Careful consultation with the board of directors or the use of organizational development consultants can help directors let go of some tasks in ways that make the best sense for the organization as a whole.

There are other creative ways to plan for the organization's future that take into account the possibility of boomer leaders' departures. For example, one group engaged in a younger generation–led long-term strategic planning process to prepare for the transfer of leadership from one generation to another. This was designed to uncover where the organization needed to strengthen its work and to help those involved—from the board to the youngest staffers—imagine how the transition might take place.

Exercise 4.2, "Thinking Five Years Ahead," on pages 91–92 is one way to help individual leaders who are remaining in the organization plan for future leadership and generational shifts. The exercise is a reminder that generational shifts are happening at all levels of the organization. This exercise can easily be integrated into a group's strategic planning process or annual assessments of goals and outcomes.

Exercise 4.2
Thinking Five Years Ahead

This exercise can be done by executive directors to create an individual action plan, but it is also useful to do in small groups of staff and board members, offering opportunities to strengthen relationships and develop a shared understanding of what needs to be done in the organization.

The first column of the table lists some concrete changes that organizations can make now that will help in future transitions. Identify how well your organization is doing in each area and what the needed next steps are.

Tasks	What Are We Doing Now?	What Are Priority Next Steps?
Staff leadership development • Recruit and support younger staff. • Make commitment to staff leadership plan. • Create opportunities for younger staff to take greater responsibilities. • Develop pathways to increased organizational leadership roles for staff members. • Encourage board members, funders, and supporters to get to know younger leaders.	• • •	• • •

(continued)

Exercise 4.2
Thinking Five Years
Ahead (*continued*)

Tasks	What Are We Doing Now?	What Are Some Priority Next Steps?
Board leadership development • Recruit and develop younger board members. • Provide board opportunities. • Involve younger board members in fundraising and meetings with donors and other supporters.	• • •	• • •
Getting ready to plan the transition • Identify resources—peers, reading, workshops, consultants—to prepare all levels of the organization. • Look for retreat or sabbatical opportunities for the executive director to step back and think about how and when to leave the organization. • Support older leaders to talk with peers about future work and movement contribution possibilities and to explore potential future options.	• • •	• • •

Changing Roles. Not all older leaders who plan to stay in their organizations want to remain in their current positions. Jan Masaoka's *The Departing: Exiting Nonprofit Leaders as Resources for Social Change* describes the different ways nonprofit executives are modifying their roles in their organizations.[3] Our interviews with boomer leaders echo her findings.

Some leaders are thinking about leadership expansion. This process is described in *ReGeneration: Young People Shaping Environmental Justice*, put out by the Movement Strategy Center.[4] Concentrating on youth organizing and environmental justice, the report suggests that founders and long-term directors are modifying their positions and finding ways to include younger generations in leadership roles. For long-term directors of smaller social sector organizations, *leadership expansion* can be a term that better aligns with their own needs than *leadership transition*.

Leadership expansion takes different forms. For example, a few groups have created a second (or more) top leadership role in the organization. A younger leader is hired to work alongside and on equal footing with a long-time leader. In another example, there have been sister organizations created that work in conjunction with, but separate from, the original group. A founder or long-time leader transitions to the new organization, which focuses on issues that are complementary to the original one. But they also give an eye to supporting younger leaders who have taken over the original organization. One leader who was in this process commented: "How do we stay active, like close enough . . . but not too close? You want to be in the movement, but you don't want to be deciding things. You want to be in a supportive role now or in a lead role but in a different area."

These older leaders are using their creativity and experience to create something new while staying involved with organizations and work where they still have a significant investment.

A Sister Organization for Elder Members

Susana Almanza is cofounder of PODER (People Organized to Defend Earth and Her Resources) in Austin, Texas. She has been working to create what she hopes will be a sister organization when she leaves PODER. While PODER focuses on youth and environmental justice issues, Susana is more aware than ever before of the many issues that are important to baby boomers and veterans of change such as health care and access to public transportation. Her idea is to start a new group organized by the older members of PODER around issues that directly affect them, while the younger leadership continues to identify the concerns related to PODER's current work. She also hopes to transition older board members of PODER into this new organization, thus leaving more room for younger leadership at PODER.

The *ReGeneration* report is careful to point out that these new arrangements require an investment of time and resources:

> The process of leadership expansion requires a deep understanding and serious time commitment, and it may take many different paths and forms. People of all ages require support for their growth and transitions within the movement. While organic and informal efforts are clearly taking place, there is a need for intentional and well-resourced structures that can better support individuals as they move into different roles in movement work.[5]

Many avenues are open to older leaders who want to remain in their organizations in addition to those described in *ReGeneration*. Some executives who stay find a new position in which they can continue to make a significant contribution in a more flexible paid position. In the Management Assistance Group (MAG), the top leader who was one of the founders has turned over her position to a new executive director but has remained an active member of the staff. MAG is now documenting their work with executive directors who are staying in organizations, describing the overall benefits of keeping on a founder or long-term chief operating officer after they give up the top position.[6]

Ways to Stay

Leaders who decide to stay in their organization may continue as the executive director. But as reported in The Departing, some executive directors are working with the organization in a different capacity—for example:

- Restructuring the executive job to be less stressful and more enjoyable, such as giving up day-to-day management by hiring a strong person as second in command or running a special project for the organization
- Fundraising or playing another role in working with major donors
- Coaching or advising staff, especially during a transition period
- Joining the board or becoming part of an advisory board
- Becoming an ambassador for the organization
- Having the former director's name remain on the organization's letterhead or other titular ways to stay affiliated
- Writing about the organization and its work[7]

Older leaders who are starting to think about their next steps are often hopeful about remaining in the group where they have invested so much of their time and energy. But they are also wary, as expressed by this founder:

When I go, could I have a connection? I wouldn't want one unless I could get out of the way . . . [but] even if I could get out of the way, do they feel I'm out of the way? . . . Is there something we could work out? But I've also seen disasters too. I think being in a position of power like the board, absolutely not, don't even go for it. But isn't there something we could be thinking about?

When consciously transferring leadership to younger generations, many older directors are surprised at the time and energy that is needed. They express a need for patience, but this plea also reveals how many older leaders are concerned about the readiness of a new generation take on more responsibility:

> We thought we could [make the transition] in a year or two, [and] change the organization. But we learned a lot of lessons from that; it can't happen that fast. Just like when you have children, it takes years of work with them to teach them things— spend time with them, nurture them. There are a lot of things that have to take place.

Leaving the top position and remaining in or close to the organization may be a trend in the future, but it is not without costs. Older leaders can find themselves pulled back into work they are trying to give up or, conversely, they may have to watch from the sidelines when they are no longer called on for their expertise. But the old paradigm that long-term leaders, especially founders, are going to walk away is being challenged by the boomers and their elders.

Leaving the Organization

With so much talk about generational transitions in leadership, it is puzzling that when an executive decides it is time to move on, the decision is so often fraught with anxiety for the organization, the board, and the individual leader. Consultants and others are helping groups by offering needed support. But change in top leadership is nothing new, and the expected departure of so many top executives should make the process more ordinary rather than something that creates a sense of crisis. There are several key elements to thinking about leadership change. Some of these are described in the discussion of executive transition management at the end of the section. Others are described below.

Before the Change. It is troubling that in nonprofit and social change work where so many people value collective action and community, older leaders feel so vulnerable. Whether this is unique to the boomer generation or a symptom of uncertain times, many of those in top positions are starting to wonder whether they will be able to leave their jobs. As one leader observed, "[We] don't know how to negotiate for ourselves. We're never going to retire. How are we ever going to get support?"

When older leaders sense that it will soon be time to go, the question is simply, How? One boomer leader assessed her generation's future in social change work by asking, "Are we the right people to actually lead the next change? Are we too entrenched in the current system? . . . I sit in a room with younger staff and trustees. And they think about the world very differently. And it's hard to take that leap of faith."

Others talk about the dangers of staying "too long" and the negative impact it can have on the organization and themselves. It can be hard to realize that you are not able to give at the same level as in earlier years. A long-time leader who decided to step down put it this way: "There were things to do. And I realized that I didn't have that energy. And I had watched colleagues who stayed way too long. And I had made my mind up several years ago that I was not going to be like that. That I could not stand to have my colleagues say, 'Oh my god, when is she going to get out of here?'"

We believe that one way to start easing the tension about planning for departure is in small groups, where older leaders can discuss how to make a decision to leave. Currently there are workshops for executives and their board members on transition planning, but there are few ongoing groups where aging leaders can find support and advice from their peers. Exercise 4.3 is one place for such a group to start but there would be plenty to talk about even without this structure.

Exercise 4.3
Taking Stock Together

Boomer executive directors would do well to seek each other out to create a supportive and safe space to talk about their future transitions. Here are some questions that can be addressed as individual reflections or in pairs or with a larger circle of executive directors when these forums are available.

Individual Reflections or Discussion in Pairs

- What am I most proud of from my tenure as the executive director (ED) of my organization?

- What are my greatest challenges as an ED now?

- When will I know that it's time for me to leave my organization? How far am I from seeing these signposts?

- What are my fears about the organization when I think about my transition?

- What are my personal concerns after leaving the organization?

Group Discussion

- How can I contribute to the social sector or social movement if I leave my organization?

- Who can help me think through these transition questions?

- Where can I find resources to help me in this process?

The advantage of group activities is they begin to take the fear and stigma out of leaving a top-level position. In addition, they can be important sources of information for those involved and for the field as well. It is here that we find out more about the particular problems that leaders have when they think about leaving their jobs. Are they concerned about a lack of recognition, fear about money, or worries about what to do next? In addition, groups can come up with new and more nuanced solutions that may be useful to others in similar positions.

In addition to staff leadership development, there is a critical need for board leadership during this transition period. One boomer commented that in many nonprofit organizations, "The culture of the board is very powerful and has the capacity to make big mistakes." Alternatively, in some organizations with a strong founder, the board can be weak. Boards have the most crucial role in this process. Not only do they hire the new leader, but they shepherd the process, starting with the way the current executive director leaves, to how a new person comes in, to how the organization adjusts to leadership changes. If they step up to the plate, all of those involved can feel respected and supported. Boards can honor a founder and welcome a new director, but sometimes it is difficult for them to do both. One young executive director told us that he followed a strong founder who had been loved by the board but also had dominated it. As the founder departed, the board suddenly became aware of its legal and fiduciary responsibility. Their anxiety about their roles and responsibilities began to express itself with the new director, who felt constantly challenged by the board. This set the stage for a protracted and difficult power struggle between the board and the new director.

The Legacy. One such aspect of leadership transition was recently identified by the Annie E. Casey Foundation, which has spearheaded much of the work on executive transition. It found that many long-time executive directors were unable to think about stepping out of their job because they were worried about the legacy they would leave.[8] In a session held at the foundation, boomer heads of Casey-funded groups talked about legacy. One noted, "Legacy thinking goes beyond, 'Am

I successful?' . . . It asks a different, more central question, 'What difference did it make?' "

Legacy raises an important and often forgotten aspect of the generational shifts in leadership. Older leaders are leaving not only their job; they are acknowledging that their work life is winding down. They are at a stage when there are fewer possibilities in the future and they may be mourning things that will never occur again for them. When we talk about the exodus of boomers, it is important to recognize that they are not simply going to another high-powered job. Instead, they are leaving that part of their life.

One boomer leader was doubtful she would ever leave the organization she founded and felt so deeply connected to. Not being at the job felt as if she would be erased. But as she explored her legacy, she could see the story of why she built this agency was already being woven into the narrative of the organization. She would be remembered by the way the staff continued to fight for children. It was then that she began to envision what it would be like to let go.

As we noted earlier, the field of executive transition management has developed to help groups think about the transition of top leaders.

Executive Transition Management

The new field of executive transition management (ETM), seeded with foundation support, offers help for organizations experiencing an executive leadership change. ETM does not replace the work of headhunters. In fact, its work often starts with groups before a transition occurs—for example, by offering services to help organizations put into place a succession plan before the executive director decides to leave as a kind of protection for emergency situations. Groups providing ETM services hold workshops on transition for nonprofit executives and

*their board members and target special needs, such as the
departure of a founder. They also train other management
support groups and consultants. ETM sees a leadership
transition as an important time in an organization.
Success is evidenced not only by finding the right person
to take over but also in preparing the organization for
change. The ETM model for organizations going through
a leadership change has three stages: prepare, pivot, thrive:*

- Prepare: *Groups need to plan for a leadership transition.
  This means working with and strengthening the board of
  directors regarding its role in hiring the new director. It
  also includes assessing the organization's strengths and
  weaknesses as well as plans for the future.*

- Pivot: *As groups search for the right replacement, the
  "pivot point" refers to supporting groups through the
  departure of the current executive director and the process
  of finding a new leader.*

- Thrive: *ETM helps the organization after a new leader
  is in place. This support takes groups through the crucial
  adjustment period after the transition has taken place.*[9]

What to Do Next: Making a Contribution

Older leaders who want to leave their positions face the inevitable question. What will they do next? Boomers are unlikely to
want to sit on the sidelines for twenty years of retirement. There
is already a considerable effort afoot to plan how the boomer
generation leaving for-profit and government jobs will contribute to the nonprofit sector, either by volunteering or taking on
paid work that is stimulating but not overly demanding.[10] But
what about exiting baby boomers who already work in the nonprofit sector? What will be their contributions?

Some departing leaders are already planning to stay involved,
and to earn additional income, by serving as interim executive

directors or in other top-level interim positions for groups experiencing leadership change. There are management service organizations that keep lists of talented former leaders to match with organizations seeking help.[11] Others leaving their jobs are interested in coaching leaders on issues ranging from vision to management. Experience Corps, a program for retirees, offers part-time and volunteer positions in nonprofits and other service-related work. With so many baby boom leaders facing full or partial retirement, it is worth exploring how to connect their skills and talents with often underresourced social change organizations and community-based organizations. These groups, unlike large service-oriented nonprofits such as Boys and Girls Clubs or the American Red Cross, are desperate for help but have few mechanisms to find and integrate experienced leaders who have time to help.

Short-term roles will be right for some, but others will seek positions that are more stable and offer benefits. Some foundations, such as the Durfee Foundation in Los Angeles, offer sabbaticals for leaders to reflect on what they have learned and to plan their next steps.[12] Another approach is the Purpose Prize, which is a $100,000 award to organizations with leaders over age sixty who have started new social entrepreneurial ventures. In this way, they recognize the creativity of older leaders. The prize, as with other Civic Venture programs, is primarily for older people entering nonprofit work from other sectors, but a similar model might be used that includes nonprofit retirees. For others, there may be discrete jobs within nonprofits for which older and experienced leaders are well suited. All these possibilities rely on individual leaders having the connections and ambition to find another position when they step down.

For leaders dedicated to social change, leading an organization is just one stop, though admittedly a long one, in their lifelong efforts to create a better world. Leaving the job is not leaving the movement. They are planning how they will contribute outside an organizational context when they continue their work after they leave their leadership jobs. Many are especially eager for a new role as they anticipate entering a period of movement building where they can contribute based on their experiences, knowledge, and skills.

Exiting social change leaders express their aspirations to stay involved in different ways. Some are interested in finding a more unified strategy for change, seeing how they can contribute by building collaborations across organizations and issues. There are leaders who are interested in returning to the basics of organizing and building a large base of constituent leaders who will be able, as one said, "to seize the movement moment." Others are hoping to contribute to the construction of a vision for what is possible in the future.

Whatever their approach, these leaders are thoughtful about making a meaningful contribution. One boomer told us,

> A number of us talked about needing to get together people sixty and older, and begin to talk about our relationship to the movement. . . . That is our common desire. I really want to do some writing—autobiography—and continue to help develop a mass-based movement.

Their knowledge and experience strengthens the next generation of social change leaders and the broader movement.

Approaching Change

The questions facing older generations about their next phase of life are not only individual issues; they are systemic. Developing pathways for older leaders to make their work and life transitions, including financial planning and emotional support, is a crucial aspect of supporting their departure. The challenges and tensions they face are not just theirs alone. With so many boomers in all sectors starting to consider what their next decades will bring, there is an obvious need for a large-scale response. The sector will have to make some wide-ranging efforts to help older generations leave and support new generations to take the lead. We explore the future for the generations that follow the boomers in the next chapter.

Notes

1. Freedman, M. *Encore: Finding Work That Matters in the Second Half of Life.* New York: Public Affairs, 2007.
2. Bridges, W. *Managing Transitions: Making the Most of Change.* (2nd ed.) Cambridge, Mass.: Da Capo Press, 2003.
3. Masaoka, J. *The Departing: Exiting Nonprofit Leaders as Resources for Social Change.* Washington, D.C.: Grantmakers for Effective Organizations, 2007.
4. Quiroz-Martinez, J., Wu, D., and Zimmerman, K. *ReGeneration: Young People Shaping Environmental Justice.* San Francisco: Movement Strategy Center, 2005.
5. Quiroz-Martinez, Wu, and Zimmerman, *ReGeneration.*
6. Conversation with Mark Leach, senior consultant for the Management Assistance Group, February 6, 2008.
7. Quiroz-Martinez, Wu, and Zimmerman, *ReGeneration.*
8. Corvington, P. *What Remains: A Consultative Session on Legacy.* Baltimore, Md.: Annie E. Casey Foundation, 2007. Some additional points were made in the facilitators memo by the Management Assistance Group.
9. See www.aecf.org/knowledgecenter/publicationseries/executivetransitionmonographs. Other examples include www.transitionguides.org, www.supportctr.org, www.compasspoint.org.
10. Zedlewski, S. *Will Retiring Boomers Form a New Army of Volunteers?* Washington, D.C.: Urban Institute, 2007; Lipton, J. "Retirement with a Purpose." *Forbes.com,* www.forbes.com/2008/01/11/volunteer-boomers-nonprofit-pf-retire_jl_0111retirement_inl.html (January 11, 2008); Salls, M. "The Nonprofit Boon from Boomers: Interview with Susan Moses." *Harvard Business School Working Knowledge,* http://hbswk.hbs.edu/archive/4416.html (October 18, 2004).

11. See Masaoka, *The Departing*.
12. The Durfee Foundation Sabbatical Program, www.durfee.org/programs/sabbatical/; Asirvatham, S. "Some Organizations That Provide Sabbatical Aid to Nonprofit Leaders." *The Chronicle of Philanthropy*, June 14, 2007, http://philanthropy.com/free/articles/v19/i17/17003802.htm; Civic Ventures' The Purpose Prize, www.purposeprize.org; Z. Smith Reynolds Foundation Sabbatical Program, www.zsr.org/sabbatical-program.

5

SOLVING THE CRISIS

A New Generation of Leaders

> I don't know how long I'll be with this particular
> group. I've also come to learn that committing
> myself to my own dreams is actually important
> too. . . . To me it's the individual change, sort of
> planting the seeds of consciousness; and I'll always
> do that.

> I see myself perhaps in the next five to ten
> years probably going into academics or perhaps
> government or foundation work. I can't keep
> twelve-hour days forever. I could probably do that
> if I was the only person in my life, but I'm not. And
> I hope to be more than just my wife and I at some
> point.

Writing in *The Nation*, Lakshmi Chaudhry speaks to the lack of
visibility of Gen Xers in progressive politics. Despite their image
as uncommitted slackers, Chaudhry claims that this cohort, across
race and gender, is redefining and revitalizing political activism.
She describes how boomers' assumptions fail to recognize that

> many of the X-ers were less lost than lost in translation, their
> rejection of politics-as-usual mistaken for apathy, their ques-
> tioning of liberal credo interpreted as "backlash" politics, their
> anxiety about economic security condemned as materialism, and

their reluctance to be identified either by labels or with larger institutions dismissed as lack of commitment.[1]

Generation X and millennials are thinking about the future of social change and planning for the decades ahead. While boomer leaders are approaching the last phase of their work careers, newer generations are watching how they move forward. Some are already established leaders; others are examining their options and opportunities.

In this chapter we turn to the future of the younger generations who are poised to take over the sector's leadership in the coming years. When we speak of the next generations, our primary focus is on Generation X, who are seeking balance in having a family, finding satisfying work, making enough money, and having an impact. Xers as a generation have been waiting to take on social sector executive positions, honing their skills and building their resumes. But given the small size of their cohort and boomer longevity, they worry that they will be usurped by millennials, a generation that resonates with boomers because of their large numbers and idealism. At the same time, both Xers and millennials are unsure whether they will take leadership in nonprofits because of the way the jobs—and the organizations—are structured.

Unlike the boomers and veterans of change, we do not have the benefit of seeing the next generation's life's work or knowing the influences that will shape their future. We do know that their world differs significantly from the one the boomers experienced at a similar age. Paradigm-busting advances in communications, technology, and science exist alongside unprecedented global challenges, such as environmental degradation, worldwide strife, and capital markets that have produced dramatic economic inequality. New leaders will be called on to demonstrate a range of hard skills, as well as the ability to integrate new knowledge and the capacity to work on local issues with large-scale thinking. They need to be flexible and thoughtful as they move forward to create social change.

Generalizing about younger people who come from two diverse generational cohorts runs the risk of not giving either generation their due. Rather than trying to present a comprehensive picture of how all Gen Xers and millennials see their future, this chapter raises the salient issues that emerged in our research and in our conversations with these cohorts as we traveled the country.

We have chosen to group these issues into four main areas: the difficulty of entering social sector organizations, the critique of boomer-led organizations, the decision to lead or not to lead, and forging new approaches to leadership.

Welcoming Organizations—Not!

Generation Xers and the first of the millennials entering the social sector are energized by working for change and participating in organizations where they can make a difference. One young staffer spoke about her work in a new organization: "I love our mission. You know, I like the fact that we get to serve this audience of people that are working really hard for making the city a better place . . . and are just fighting for . . . a better world."

Despite the commitment to social sector work, younger generation staffers also have ambivalent feelings based on their experiences on the job. They find many organizations indifferent to their contributions and criticize groups that operate in ways that seem to contradict their social change values. Newer generations feel loyal to a change agenda, but their experiences in individual organizations often leave them confused about their role.

SOA: Stuck on Arrival

The first encounter with social sector organizations is often the most formative. We found new staffers entering nonprofit work excited by the opportunity of turning service-learning, internships, summer jobs, or volunteer work into a paid position. But unlike boomer activists, who were grateful for the chance to earn a living at something they loved and be part of something new, Generation Xers talked about the disappointment of being tracked into low-level administrative positions in existing organizations, where neither their enthusiasm nor their skills were put to good use.

Many small and midsize groups hire young college graduates into entry-level jobs. New generations benefit by getting a foot in the door and organizations gain eager and hard-working staffers. But there is often a miss. After the thrill of finding a position, Next Geners often find themselves stuck. They accept positions that do not take advantage of their education and abilities assuming they will be included in a larger team effort to address important issues. Many hope that good performance at even low-level jobs can lead to more responsible positions. But neither option may be available.

Most groups are not structured to take advantage of the untapped skills of entry-level staffers. There is little incentive for already overwhelmed groups to invest in young employees who are providing essential services but who will leave in a year or two to go back to school or move to another organization. But new staffers, even if they leave, would like to feel that their ideas and contributions are recognized. They don't just want to be treated nicely by boomer executives (though this helps); they are looking to make a difference. And so, after a year or two, they move on to another job, often disappointed by their experience.

Organizational Malaise

As Generation Xers age, they find their way into midlevel positions where they run programs, oversee administrative tasks, raise funds, and take on a host of other responsibilities. Many find they are often unable to move up even after years of experience in groups where boomers dominate the top spots. Squeezed between powerful long-time leaders and eager millennial staffers who want to change the way things are done, older Gen Xers often feel their own ideas and ambitions overlooked, and over time, they can become disgruntled. One Gen X program director told us he thought about taking over if the current executive director decided to leave. Yet he was hesitant:

> I don't know if I want the baggage that comes along with being the ED of this organization, unless there was a serious turnover of staff in the hierarchy, where that would give you more of an ability to try to start fresh. But you have certain ideas and attitudes that are just embedded and ingrained in the institution of [the organization] that would be extremely difficult to change.

In some groups, long-term leaders have left unaddressed long-term internal problems such as ineffective programs or overworked staffers as long as funding comes in and the organization continues to function. Boards seem unaware of the concerns and may also be in need of revamping. Newer generations quickly learn that the culture resists change. The stability at the top masks dysfunction below that keeps younger leaders and their ideas from making an impact on the work.

Generation Xers and millennials in social change work also complain of groups where internal decision making is unclear, roles and responsibilities confusing, and the meaning of delivering on mission elusive. They learn there are differences between the formal organization and the way power is actually exercised, and they express frustration at what they see as managerial disorder and bad habits that hinder a group's health and effectiveness.

As a result of these experiences, newer generations try to find other jobs in organizations that they feel share their values or at least will provide them with more opportunity. Moving to different groups for better jobs is a logical way to build a career, but the discouragement with feeling left out or overlooked by organizations and their leadership can cause a kind of rancor that diminishes the good feelings that accompany social change work.

In addition, Gen Xers and millennials are willing to try other sectors in hopes of finding a better fit in either public institutions or for-profit organizations. One young leader who ended up in a high-end consulting firm was amazed, and delighted, at the type of training and attention he received.

Questioning Organizations

The disillusionment some Next Geners feel in the sector may be less of a problem with individual boomer leaders than with the culture that has developed within organizations over time. There is a certain acceptance of how things operate that makes sense to long-timers but is questioned by new generations.

Who Decides: Internal Operations, External Values

One of the tensions that face social sector organizations is the balance between organizational survival and acting on mission. How this equilibrium is calibrated can be different for younger generations coming into nonprofit work and those who have been at it for decades. An area that is particularly difficult for new staffers is the contradictions that arise between a group's espoused principles and its internal organizational practice. Younger generations want to make the world a better place, and they expect that starts at home, that is, within the organization. Older leaders feel their good work stands on its own and do not want to spend precious time examining how well internal operations are aligning with the staffs' views of the mission and vision.

In one example, a Generation Xer was charged with writing the reports for his unit in a well-respected research group. He worked hard and was happy to have a job where his thinking was valued. However, when he noticed editing on his reports that omitted or reworded findings because they did not support the policy views of the organization, he became cynical. His supervisor sympathized, but, he was told, the leader of the organization had made the changes, so there was nothing to be done.

Others find the decision-making process confusing and unsatisfactory. Many older leaders are committed to run organizations that are inclusive of staff members' ideas. However, new generations frequently experience this inclusion as confusion. For example, Generation X staffers were exasperated by the idea of hierarchy "with input," which they found long on process and short on transparency. In one group, a young employee was tired of long meetings where everyone gave their opinion and then felt the decisions rarely reflected the group's input. The story in "Who Makes Decisions?" demonstrates how leaders are often unaware of how staffers feel about their decision-making structures.

Who Makes Decisions?

A young staffer said that in his organization, the boomer codirectors asked for ideas during staff meetings. There would be great conversation, but later the staff would find out that the final decision was completely different from what was discussed at their meetings. The staff members spent a lot of time and energy offering their ideas and opinions, but in their view, they rarely had an impact on what actually happened. When a facilitator came to help with some organizational planning, she put a table in the middle of the room and said, "I am inviting someone to use the chairs to show us where everybody is 'at the table' in this organization." One of the young staff members got up. He put a few chairs at the table, representing the directors and long-time senior staff. Then he placed chairs at varying distances from the table: some off in a corner, some facing the wall, some out in the hallway. The other staff applauded his description, but the long-time directors were shocked. The exercise was a major eye-opener for those in charge of the organization.

Younger generations may come into existing groups with high ideals, but they can quickly become jaded. The result is cynicism about leadership and power. Ron Carucci noticed a similar phenomenon in the corporate sector. In *Leadership Divided,* he observes that many "enthusiastic, eager, outrageously smart" Gen Xers are interested in leading. The catch is, 'they have no desire whatsoever to lead as they have been led.' "[2]

To Be Seen and Heard

The aspirations of Generation Xers and millennials are also dampened when they are overlooked as leadership material. Younger generations in the social sector who want to take on more leadership find they are unable to get the attention of boomer bosses, who appear to be more comfortable with their own cohort. Older leaders value Generation Xers and millennials for their expertise in areas such as finance, policy analysis, management, and technology. But younger generations often feel that their abilities to think big and develop strategy, outcomes, and vision are overlooked.

Some think boomer leaders simply don't recognize leadership styles that are different from their own. Deborah Seigel aptly describes this discrepancy in the women's movement in *Sisterhood Interrupted.* While boomer feminists fought for recognition and new institutions to promote women, younger generations enter with new and different ideas of what constitutes women's issues—ideas that older women do not agree with and feel negate their own struggles. As a result, both cohorts are disappointed. Younger women coming into "feminist" organizations express disappointment that claims of inclusion ring false.

> Young women coming up within the ranks of women-run institutions accused older women of hypocrisy, charging them with hoarding—instead of sharing—power. . . . Senior women who knew

how to negotiate office politics with men . . . had a difficult time, it seemed, negotiating power differentials with junior women.[3]

Older leaders worked hard for their power and are not letting it go with ease. They feel that younger generations will never understand the battles they fought. Boomers define social change leadership from their own experiences and in ways that make sense to their generation. As younger cohorts challenge these assumptions, friction arises between generations.

Younger leaders feel in a bind. If they pay their elders the respect that is their due, they fear they will have to give up the ideas they think are relevant now. If they push their ideas, they are viewed as arrogant and ungrateful. As one Gen Xer explained, "[The boomers] may have mentored us around a passion for the work we do, but didn't necessarily know how to help us put it together or make it work."

Exercise 5.1 is one way to approach some of these conflicts. It teaches different age cohorts to see these diverse perspectives as an opportunity.

Exercise 5.1
Looking at Our Assumptions:
What We Think; What They Think

This is an exercise to use with a small or large group that has representatives from different generations.

Step 1

Divide the group by generations, and ask each group to fill out the table that follows. Provide enough time to fully discuss all four columns for each issue (about twenty minutes).

Step 2

Bring the groups together to share their responses.

(continued)

**Exercise 5.1
Looking at Our Assumptions:
What We Think; What They
Think (*continued*)**

Step 3

Debrief the activity by asking the following questions:

- What have you learned about each other's responses?

- What assumptions were made by each generation about the other generation?

- What's one generational difference in ideas or leadership style that you would like to turn into a mutual learning opportunity in your own work?

Key Difference in Ideas or Leadership Style Among Baby Boomers, Gen Xers, and Millennials	Why Do You Think This Difference Exists?	What Else Could This Difference Mean?	How Can This Difference Be Turned into a Mutual Learning Opportunity? What Are the First Steps Needed?
1.			
2.			
3.			
4.			

(Not) Speaking About Race

In Chapter One, we noted that younger staff of color feel particularly invisible as leaders in the social sector. Many communities of color are served by nonprofits, but leaders of color in social sector organizations are scarce. Ironically, Next Geners of color are more likely to aspire to become executive directors than their white counterparts.[4]

In predominantly white organizations, younger leaders of color struggle with taking on power and keeping their identity. This is especially true when there are few other people of color in leadership. "The big challenge for me," said one young person, "was having been one of the first people of color in a white organization and one of the first people of color that stuck with it long enough to actually develop an aspiration to have power in the organization."

There is a different sort of pressure when Next Geners of color work in race-based organizations led by older leaders. Here, younger people of color may challenge existing paradigms without the credentials of living through the civil rights and other identity-based power movements that defined their elders' lives. Despite their respect for these older leaders, they feel frustrated by the resistance to new ideas and new leadership styles. For example, some younger people of color working in single-race groups talk about trying to open organizations to consider more multicultural perspectives. Others note the gender bias they face or what they see as outdated views on sexual orientation and identity. Though these same issues occur in white-run organizations, younger people of color feel the extra pressure of negotiating multiple identities in a changing world.

Nonprofits as the Problem

Among younger activists, questions are also being raised about the very role of nonprofit organizations. Branding the sector as the "nonprofit-industrial complex," this group argues that, like the military-industrial complex or the prison-industrial complex, the money and energy that go into running nonprofit organizations divert them from making social change.[5] Mentored by older activists who have worked in the sector, these builders for a new movement believe that funds from elite foundations and government keep groups from making a significant challenge to the status quo.

Those who have lost faith in nonprofits, even if they still work in these organizations, hope to find alternative ways for funding movement building for social change. Ideally the support would come from the communities that are active in and benefit from social change activities. One millennial leader who codirects a social change group talked about the importance of not banking on a career as a nonprofit leader. She was looking ahead to a time when she would have a job that was not directly related to her movement-building activities; then her paid work would not constrain her actions toward restructuring society.

What It Takes to Lead

> If I read the news today with my heart wide open and my mind engaged, I will be crushed. Do I address the injustices in Sudan, Iraq, Burma, Pakistan, the Bronx? Do I call an official, write a letter, respond to a MoveOn.org request? None of it promises to be effective and it certainly won't pacify my outrage.

Courtney Martin, quoted above, chafes at accusations that she and other millennials are less active or committed to social change than other generations. Martin thinks her generation is overwhelmed with stories of "torture, murder, and blatant disregard for our civil liberties and environmental health."[6]

The complexity and scale of problems new generations of social change leaders will face have led younger leaders to think carefully about what will sustain them so that they will be able to rise to the challenges of the coming decades. Three areas are particularly important: focusing on renewal, finding fair compensation, and redefining leadership jobs.

Renewal for the Long Haul. Generation Xers and millennials recognize that the fight for systemic change is a battle that will be long and difficult, and they want to prevent the burnout and cynicism they have witnessed in older leaders. Younger leaders talk about the need for spiritual renewal and self-care, not because they are afraid to work hard, but because they want to prepare themselves, mentally and physically, for their commitment to social change work over a lifetime. "It's really important to take care of ourselves and not work ourselves to death," said one Gen Xer.

The increased attention to personal well-being is one way new generations are addressing the toll that social sector work takes on staff. Although the work draws on people's passion and desire for change, it also exposes them to the depth of problems. Spirituality or faith has been one way to sustain energy for transforming the world despite seemingly insurmountable obstacles as evidenced by Martin Luther King Jr., Mahatma Gandhi, and Malcolm X.

But as the social sector has become more professionalized, less attention has been paid to how staff and leaders are replenished in order to continue their work. Instead, there is increasing pressure to produce, accompanied by an assumption that the good fight, and good outcomes, will be reward enough. But in an era when winning is not always possible, professionals and activists can easily burn out without some additional systemic support. The *Stepping Up or Stepping Out* report found that among young nonprofit professionals planning to leave the sector, burnout, at 90 percent, was the top reason.[7] So it is no surprise that many younger leaders are turning to renewal as a way to cope with the stress and demands of nonprofit work.

Several new organizations are making the connections between spirituality and social change work. Spirit in Action brings together social change activists in their local communities to talk about four core strategies: connecting with spirit, healing from divisions, visioning the future, and taking action for deep and long-term change. Stone Circles has a fellowship program that supports work in spiritual activism and conducts workshops in this area as well. Selah provides Jewish social justice leaders with training by pairing with the Rockwood Leadership Institute. Programs such as Windcall Institute and Vallecitos Mountain Refuge offer social justice activists and nonprofit leaders opportunities for individual renewal through residencies in outdoor settings and a chance to unplug from daily demands.[8]

Stone Circles Paradigm

At its best, this new paradigm, which some of us are calling "spiritual activism" or "liberation spirituality" is revolutionary. It provides us with deepened competencies and tools to go forward in this tangle of conditions history has prepared for us and to assume the roles we're being asked to play. While the field growing up around this new paradigm is varied and vast, we are beginning to see each other and understand what we share:

- *A deep commitment to spiritual life and practice*
- *A framework of applied liberation*
- *An orientation towards movement-building and*
- *A desire for fundamental change in the world based on equity and justice.*[9]

Leadership development programs are also focusing on self-care as an essential part of their training. Physical and mental health, from the food we eat to the need for exercise, to an endorsement of vacations, are emphasized as important pieces of both being a role model and staying in leadership for the long haul.

Social Justice Leadership Collaborative: The Skills of Renewal

When Ng'ethe Maina came to New York City, he had already been a community organizer and a supervisor to groups of organizers for many years, and he knew firsthand about burnout. So before coming to the city, he participated in a leadership program that redirected his energy to focus on his purpose and renewed his spirit. The experience was transformational, and he realized that others who were working for social change could use something similar.

Ng'ethe founded Social Justice Leadership, which offers intensive training programs to help leaders,

> *especially those heading organizing groups, increase their ability to be visionary, compassionate, and effective. The program supports leaders to build relationships with each other and offers them new skills, with a heavy emphasis on self-reflection and renewal. One leader who is part of the program commented, "I thought when I first attended, 'What is all this meditation about? What are we going to do?' But now I see how the process really builds ourselves and our relationships with each other."*

The Movement Strategy Center offers services to nonprofit groups such as alliance building, organizational development, field development, and the Spirit in Motion Program, which works to support a balanced approach to work and life.

Helping to replenish social change leaders and staff members is one aspect of maintaining them in the work. But accompanying spiritual well-being are more material concerns as well.

Fair Compensation. Generation Xers and millennials are in the workforce at a time very different from the boomer and veterans of change generations. The cost of living has increased, and younger generations are often struggling with expenses and debts from education loans, credit cards, and housing costs.[10] Elizabeth Warren and Amelia Warren Tyagi found that in the United States today, two-earner middle-class families pay 75 percent of their income to fixed costs, such as housing, health care, transportation, and taxes, compared to the 54 percent that was paid by one-income earning households a generation ago. This, combined with an unregulated credit card industry, has made today's earners, even those in two-wage families, at higher risk for financial problems.[11] It is not only salaries that concern newer generations; they also worry about health-care coverage, contributions to retirement plans, and paid leave time—and at a time when groups are cutting back to save costs rather than increasing these benefits.

Many of those concerned about the leadership crisis have endorsed the need to boost salaries of nonprofit executives. In fact, salaries of nonprofit leaders have been rising over the past ten years, and for a small number of people running very large organizations, compensation packages have been viewed as excessive, mirroring some of the problems seen in the for-profit world.[12] But for many executive directors, especially in small and midsized organizations, adequate compensation remains an issue.

One of the problems is that the concern about pay is not simply an executive issue. In some states, living wage campaigns are fought by nonprofit groups that rely on low-wage work to provide services for clients. Raising compensation for top positions may simply reinforce the large differential in earnings between leaders and staff members, a practice that reflects poorly on social sector organizations and turns away younger staffers. The financial divide is especially problematic for groups that work primarily with low-income and other marginalized people. High executive pay raises questions about how money is spent and the distance between leaders, staffers, and the community.

The solution is not simply raising the salary of top leadership but to look at ways that the sector as a whole needs to revamp its salary structure. For years, leaders have kept organizations alive by accepting funding that undermines the sector's ability to pay decent wages. This practice is being questioned by a new generation that is committed to social change but is also saddled with debt and faced with increased costs of living. Social sector organizations and their funders need to set realistic financial goals that include fair compensation for all levels of staff. In addition, groups can identify sectorwide approaches to how to save costs. For example, smaller groups can come together to share back office expenses, enhance benefits, and reduce rising liabilities.[13] Attacking student debt is an important factor in reducing the financial burdens of those entering nonprofit work. The Nonprofit Sector Workforce Coalition has proposed a federal student loan forgiveness program as part of their larger goal of attracting recent college graduates to nonprofit jobs.

More intentional action on the issues of compensation for social sector work is needed to recalibrate the real costs of the work and pressure organizational leaders and funding sources to respond to legitimate salary concerns raised by younger generations.

Redefining Leadership Jobs. Renewal and remuneration will help new generations with the challenges of social change work, but they do not solve the problem of the work that the top leadership positions demand. Gen Xers and millennials are unsure if they can follow in the footsteps of executive directors, who are able to keep organizations going by what appears to be sheer will. Many younger leaders are interested in retooling these jobs, but they need board and funder support to succeed.

One way to encourage a new look at executive positions is in Exercise 5.2, which can be done individually but is better suited for a group. The purpose of the exercise is to do a realistic assessment of what the executive director's role entails. This sort of documentation, which can also be done with senior managers or other positions, provides invaluable information about what the job involves. Executive directors and boards can work together on what can be done to relieve executives of unneeded burdens.

Exercise 5.2
Top Leadership: Defining the Job

Complete the chart with specific roles, tasks, and time needed to do the tasks. We listed some suggestions to get you started, but you know best what the tasks are in your organization. Then complete the final column about who can do this task. As much as possible, identify someone else in the organization who can do the tasks.

There are many aspects of an executive director's job that cannot be adequately captured in a task-oriented way, such as helping to define and move forward the vision and building and maintaining relationships. Nevertheless, taking these steps to list and identify responsibilities is a starting point to acknowledge what an executive director is required to do and in what ways this work can be shared by others in the organization.

(continued)

Exercise 5.2
Top Leadership: Defining the Job (*continued*)

Job Responsibilities	What Is Needed	Time Needed (or Percentage of Time Needed)	Who Else Can Do It
Reporting to the board of directors	• Board reports three times a year • Weekly conversation with board chair • Board committee meetings • Board fundraising plan follow-up	• Two weeks notice for project leaders; one day editing; two days getting out	• Project leaders write reports, executive director reviews, administrative assistant puts report together • Prepare for calls, have discussion about board
Financial oversight	•	•	•
Creating the annual budget	•	•	•
Raising funds	• Developing fundraising plan • Meeting with foundations • Writing proposals • Meeting with government • Meeting with individual donors	• •	• •

Job Responsibilities	What Is Needed	Time Needed (or Percentage of Time Needed)	Who Else Can Do It
Overseeing all grants and reporting requirements	•	•	•
Overseeing all staff	• Promote clear communication of desires and healthy work practices	•	• Work with supervisors
Overseeing programs	• Ensure program alignment with mission and long-term strategy	•	•
Attend meetings and conferences	• Represent the organization locally and nationally	•	• Associate director or program directors as appropriate; board members
Strategic planning	•	•	•

Being clear about the responsibilities of the executive director is the first step in understanding whether or not the job is really doable. It also helps the director and the board identify whether more staff is needed or if some of the responsibilities can be shifted to others in the organization. It is not uncommon for executive directors to find that their jobs are divided into two parts when they leave. Why not figure out how to prepare for this change while the current leader is still in the position?

To Lead or Not to Lead

In many ways, older social sector leaders forged their own positions based on what was needed to survive through a changing external environment. Over time, these jobs were fitted to these boomer leaders, even with all their demands and challenges. The irony is that older leaders, who have worked so hard to build their organizations, have inadvertently created a model of leadership that younger generations feel equates leading social sector organizations with giving up personal well-being.

Based on their experiences, it is no wonder that Gen Xers and millennials are ambivalent about taking a top leadership position in established organizations. They are working hard to remain in the sector, but beyond their feeling of rejection and stress, what new generations seem to fear most is the formula that they have to give up life balance and in some cases financial security to take on social sector leadership.

At the same time older leaders who love their work are looking to cut down on their hours by ridding themselves of the parts of the job they dislike such as administrative tasks or staff supervision. Yet, why would Generation X and millennials want to take positions that focus on tasks current leaders are trying to shed?

New generations will have to decide if they want to take on the responsibility and power of leadership, and find ways to make it work for their generation. The path they will take to become leaders will certainly differ from older generations as is appropriate given the changes that have occurred in the past decades.

Alternative Pathways to Leadership

In the *Ready to Lead* study, one-third of the respondents reported they had aspirations to be an executive; only 11 percent would not even consider the possibility. Those aspiring to leadership are preparing by obtaining the skills they need, focusing both on the hard skills such as finance, management, public speaking, and fundraising and the soft skills of building networks and connections.[14] In addition, they are finding ways to ready themselves for the demands of long-term social change work.

Steps for Advancement and Skills Building. Newer generations recognize that they need to create pathways within the sector for moving up in their organizations or to positions of leadership elsewhere. Generation X has pursued obtaining academic credentials in management, and it is likely that millennials also will turn to school as a way to prepare for leadership roles.[15] Although they were not always sure what types of degrees to pursue, over half of the respondents to a survey conducted by Emily Davis thought that formal education was "an important tool in advancing their nonprofit careers."[16]

Next Geners also take advantage of training opportunities at work. Almost two-thirds of respondents in *Ready to Lead* reported their organizations gave them access to professional development activities. Skills training programs reward staffers and fill in for what organizational leaders either do not have time or do not know how to teach. In addition, younger generations who come from less elite backgrounds can take advantage of opportunities that will bring them up to speed with those who enter the work with more educational benefits.

There has also been a marked expansion of programs specifically focused on building leadership capacity in the social sector. The Leadership Learning Community Web site lists over seventy nonprofit leadership programs in the United States.[17] These programs range from leadership support for executive directors to skills building for staffers interested in taking on top-level positions. For example, as a result of a study of leadership transitions in New York City funded by the United Way, a partnership was formed among three organizations to build leadership capacity at all levels. They have created a multitiered program that includes staff and board members as well as current executive directors.

Building Leadership

One approach that is more field oriented is taking place in New York City where the local United Way is partnering with Baruch College School of Public Affairs and the Support Center for Nonprofit Management to build new leadership (www.unitedwaynyc.org). They offer four programs that "provide a diverse group of professionals with the skills, connections and credentials necessary to lead, either as a nonprofit employee or as a board member":

- Junior Fellows: *A twelve-week program that provides a strong foundation in management theory and practice for those with two or more years of nonprofit experience.*

- Senior Fellows: *A two-semester one-year program (with academic credit) for those with five or more years of experience to learn the skills to advance to an executive position.*

- Executive Fellows: *For those already directing organizations to enhance their leadership skills through assessment, peer learning, coaching, and conversations with experts in the field.*

- Linkages Board Training and Placement: *Recruits, trains, and places new board members for nonprofit groups. The program also maintains a strong alumni network.*

Organizations that want to build and retain younger leaders can use external programs and offer internal support. One method described in Charan, Dortter, and Noel's *The Leadership Pipeline* explains how staffers need proper preparation both before and after they are promoted. According to the authors, organizational leadership is developed intentionally and in stages. For example, to help younger leaders gain more skills, supervisors can "provide carefully selected job assignments that stretch people over time and allow them to learn and process necessary skills."[18]

It is a cycle of stretching staff to prepare for the next level, promoting them into new jobs with more authority and responsibility, and then actively supporting them to be successful in their new position before the cycle starts again. Smaller groups can offer challenging tasks that raise staffers' decision-making and other skills even if there are not specific ways to advance given the size of the organization. These staff members may eventually leave their jobs for a better position and they will carry with them the knowledge of how to help others grow and find a positive experience working in nonprofit organizations. The payoff is the strengthening of the sector and former employees who remain loyal to the organization that invested in them wherever they may work.

Mentoring. Readying new generations for leadership through training and development provides them with skills and information. But this is only half of the equation. Staffers move to new positions based on their competencies, but they also are hired because of their relationship to trusted colleagues who can vouch for their abilities. Mentors and networks provide Generation Xers and millennials with information about jobs, the connections they need to get their foot in the door, and the legitimacy that they are truly leadership material.

Much of the talk about advancing new generations is about mentors. In the study of young nonprofit professionals in Colorado, over half had mentors, and 94 percent found this relationship helped to advance their career.[19] Although there are programs that focus on skills development, mentoring offers newer generations a way into the leadership circle dominated by older cohorts.

For young leaders, a mentor is someone who gives a sense of perspective and history, offers advice, and shares contacts and influence. Studies on mentoring in for-profits show that younger leaders with mentors are more likely to advance, earn higher salaries, and report more satisfaction with their work.[20] In the nonprofit sector, mentoring is not only useful on the job but helps to shape new leaders' vision and goals.

Older leaders also benefit from mentoring relationships. They learn what younger generations think and gain insights from new ideas about the work. The relationship also gives older leaders the opportunity to help a new generation carry on their good work.

Finding mentoring that works for both older leaders and those who are younger is not always easy. In some cases, younger generations report that their mentors are more interested in power brokering than power sharing, as in this case:

> "There's a mentor who's really there to help you and develop your skills—and there's the one that sees you as a piece of their empire and wants to create you in their model. We think mentoring is good, but there needs [to be] a consistent mentoring process."

Mentors advising young leaders as a way to expand their own sphere of influence can be a way of grooming a new generation while passing on old animosities between rival organizations and ideas. Gen Xers are baffled by these divisions that were set in motion decades ago. New generations are interested in the history, but not in repeating it.

Mentoring can also be fraught with the issue of power. The power that comes with age, experience, and relationships seems to be what younger people want access to, but it can also cause resentment—for example, one younger leader commented, "When I go to funders, . . . everyone asks me who my mentor is. I've learned to expect it; eventually everyone asks. It's like, 'Who taught you and should we let you in?'"

An entrée for some, mentoring regimes can also result in setting barriers for others, especially for women and people of color who may not be recognized by older generations as leadership material. Overall, mentoring works best when the benefits for both the older and younger partners in the relationship are defined and the power of both generations is clear. Older leaders have experience and networks built over a lifetime of work. New generations bring access to new trends and innovative ways of approaching problems. Good mentoring partnerships recognize and encourage both of these aspects of their relationship.

What It Takes: Improving Mentoring Relations

DEFINE THE RELATIONSHIP

Mentoring has a mystique about it that can hinder the development of the relationship. We imagine the one perfect person who will guide us throughout our career, offering us invaluable advice and paving the road for our success. But in a Harvard case note, Beyond the Myth of the Perfect Mentor: Building a Network of Developmental Relationships, *the authors remind us that mentoring is an exchange relationship that benefits both parties. It is often short term, and most people have many mentoring relationships over their career.*[21] *Based on these findings, it is important to discard preconceived ideas about mentoring and think about what the relationship can bring to both parties.*

CLARIFY EXPECTATIONS

In a mentoring relationship between generations, both sides need to be clear about their expectations. There is nothing more frightening to older leaders who are already overworked to think they will be called on to mentor eager young colleagues. And there is nothing more disappointing to younger leaders who think they are going to get valuable information than to find their relationships consist mostly of occasional lunches with mentors who regale them with stories of the good old days. The mentoring relationship can be useful and interesting to both parties, but it needs to have boundaries and mutual expectations of what is being exchanged.

Pay Attention to Race

Young people of color have more difficulty finding mentors in their work. The research on race and mentoring indicates that this is not simply an issue for those working in nonprofits. People of color coming into the workforce are less likely to have mentors, especially mentors of color. Some studies in business show new M.B.A.s of color have two sets of mentors: white mentors at work who provide access and people of color mentors outside the job who provide support.[22] Older leaders of all races need to be sensitive to the difficulties young leaders of color have in these relationships and provide needed support.

Teach Older Leaders

When older nonprofit leaders decide to mentor younger employees, they are often at a loss. They want to provide something that is useful, but since many of them were never mentored, they do not know how. We often assume that someone in a position of power and authority should have these skills, so we neglect to teach them how to mentor. Accessible information and materials are needed so that older leaders can learn how to be good and productive mentors to new generations.

Stepping Up: New Wine, Old Skins

Not all concerns about leading rest on older generations. Some younger leaders express frustration that their own generation shies away from accepting power, and others claim the problem lies in the way power is exercised. As one Gen Xer expressed it,

> It is as important that people who are participating in a collaborative organization know how to participate as it is that the leader knows how to lead. . . . You have to know what it means to share

responsibilities, to step up and participate, to not wait for your leader to tell you what to do. You have to build your own capacity to participate so that when a leader says, "Here's an opportunity for you to take leadership," you know how to step into that. And you feel confident to say to your leader, "I'm not comfortable with how this decision's being made."

Younger directors struggle with ways to operate that challenge people to do their best work and make a lasting impact, especially when they take on organizations in which existing operations, decision making, and board expectations are based on the style of previous executive directors. Newer leaders are looking for organizational alignment of the work they do, more widespread participation in decision making, and more transparency in operations. But how to accomplish this is often no more apparent to new leaders than it was to older ones:

I think the leadership challenge is often to balance the whole idea of visions and thinking big and growing and dreaming with the reality of where your organization is, and building the infrastructure and taking the time to focus, and building the capacity to help get the people in the organization to those places. And to be sure that the vision is always the vision that everyone is buying into. That's a big challenge.

The pressure of keeping organizations running and rethinking internal structures, especially in established organizations, makes it hard to figure out effective decision-making practices that alleviate rather than burden the work. Without support for these changes, new leaders can easily get discouraged, as this Gen Xer noted: "One of the challenges of being a director was trying to experiment with process. After three years, I'm kind of over it. I'm kind of back into hierarchy and knowing what everybody needs to do. I don't know how I feel about that, I don't know that I like that."

New generations' views of nonprofit leadership are not uniform. As they move into leadership roles, they are looking for information and support that will make it possible to stay.

Forging New Approaches: Leading Organizations

The leadership challenge for new generations is often less about leadership style than about how to operate organizations in a new way. We describe four approaches that newer leaders, and sometimes older ones, are taking to change the structure of leadership, the decision-making process, or the culture within organizations:

- Embracing social entrepreneurship
- Running a group with more than one top leader
- Using participatory decision making
- Distributing leadership throughout the organization

These models are not new and they are not the only innovations being tried, but they are examples of how next-generation leaders are eager to reinvent structures to make working in nonprofits both rewarding internally and effective in the external world. Some groups we talked with used more than one of the approaches described here or mixed in more traditional structures with newer ones in their search for the right combination for their organization.

Embracing Social Entrepreneurship

Many Generation Xers and millennials, especially those with an elite education, are drawn to starting their own organizations. They are entrepreneurial and ready to act on an idea of how to make change. Their experience with older leaders is they are slow to take action and often uninterested in these new ideas. Social entrepreneurs are one type of post-boomer leadership. They move on their own dreams and think big. They believe that one person, or one idea, can change the world. Rather than wait for recognition from a generation that they feel faltered at delivering on its promise for a new society, they are seeking funders who are ready to invest, and those who share similar viewpoints and approaches.

On the Web sites of various social entrepreneurial fellowship programs, names appear such as Maria Montessori, who started the Montessori school movement, and Muhammad Yunus, the 2006 Nobel Peace Prize winner, head of Grameen Bank, and credited with the spread of microlending for low-income women throughout the world. They also mention Yale graduate Wendy Kopp, who started Teach for America in 1990, a two-year commitment for college grads to teach in a public school in a low-income community, and Jane Addams, who in 1889 at the age of twenty-nine started a movement when she founded the first settlement house in the United States where middle-class women and men lived cooperatively in low-income neighborhoods to share knowledge and culture with the urban poor.[23]

Descriptions of Social Entrepreneurs

Ashoka: "*Social entrepreneurs are individuals with innovative solutions to society's most pressing social problems. They are ambitious and persistent, tackling major social issues and offering new ideas for wide-scale change.*" (*www.ashoka.org*)

echoing green: "*we believe that there is nothing more powerful for realizing social change than a powerful new idea in the hands of a true social entrepreneur.*

"*The entrepreneurial spirit that has long driven the economic growth in the U.S and around the world needs to be brought to the social sector.*" (*www.echoinggreen.org*)

> Skoll Foundation: *"Entrepreneurs have always been
> the drivers of progress. In the business world, they
> act as engines of growth, harnessing opportunity and
> innovation to fuel economic advancement. Social
> entrepreneurs, like their business brethren, are similarly
> focused; they tap into vast reserves of ambition,
> creativity and resourcefulness in relentless pursuit of
> hard, measurable results. But social entrepreneurs
> seek to grow more than just profits. Motivated by
> altruism and a profound desire to promote the growth
> of equitable civil societies, social entrepreneurs pioneer
> innovative, effective, sustainable approaches to meet
> the needs of the marginalized, the disadvantaged and the
> disenfranchised. Social entrepreneurs are the wellspring
> of a better future."* (www.skollfoundation.org)

The entrepreneur's interest in making big change and getting results is appealing to many Generation Xers and millennials who grew up in a period of wide-scale technological change fueled by entrepreneurial ventures. Social entrepreneurs identify investors, often from the world of venture capitalists, who lend not only their money but also their business skills to help organizations take an idea to scale in order to have maximum impact. Some social entrepreneurs have already made fortunes in for-profit ventures and are now hoping to use those skills to address social problems.

The focus in the entrepreneurial organization is on the individual leader rather than on the type of organization run or the decision-making process.[24] For those put off by more formal structures, there is an excitement and energy in these organizations. The staff is part of something new that has a large vision and looks for tangible results. In their initial start-up years, bureaucracy is minimized in order to get things done and ensure immediate impact.

Older-generation nonprofit leaders and young social entre-preneurs working toward the same goals often do not even speak the same language. New leaders are learning from business about market share and going to scale; older leaders are reflect-ing back on their own hopes of creating a better world, talking about social change and tempered by experience. For one group, movement building evokes demonstrations on the streets; for the other building a movement brings up images of branding, capitalization, and return on investment.

Of course, not all Gen Xers and millennials are social entre-preneurial converts. There are those who are skeptical of rely-ing on business ideas, especially when addressing social issues that cannot be measured by the bottom line. Some worry that social entrepreneurs come from elite backgrounds, testing their concepts on poor and other marginalized populations. But even those who reject the language and behaviors of entrepreneurs are open to ideas that come from business leaders, especially when it comes to running organizations. In fact, 78 percent of the *Ready to Lead* respondents have worked in the corporate sector. And despite misgivings, the entrepreneurial model has great appeal, especially to Generation X and millennials, for its emphasis on a large vision and pragmatic solutions.

Leading Together

Many Gen X social change leaders who do not embrace entre-preneurship have moved in a different direction. They are more interested in sharing leadership, building more on the experi-ences of some of the movement organizations of the 1960s and 1970s than on current business operations. There are also newer leaders who are trying structures such as codirectors, leadership teams, or other variations of sharing the top responsibility. Some groups form executive teams that operate with communal lead-ership even if there is a formal executive director.

It makes sense that sharing the top spot would appeal to new generations. Whereas boomer leadership sharing often resulted in power struggles, Generation Xers and millennials are frequently recognized for their comfort in working in teams and even shying away from power.[25] Shared leadership offers the ability to distribute the load of responsibilities that can weigh heavily on one person. There is built-in support when difficult issues arise, ranging from raising money to staff management to board relations. Joint leadership gives those involved the sense that they are making better decisions by having varying points of view at the top level. In addition, executives can take some time away from work for parental leave or sabbaticals without fear that the organization will fall apart in their absence.

One organization with a leadership team started with the cofounders and then expanded to include another person on staff to diversify the leadership group. The organization is characterized by a common vision, a high level of internal communication, meaningful staff meetings, and individual support for staffers, who are all under forty years old. The group has high standards for success based on solid performance measures. Staffers are deeply committed and work long hours, even making themselves available after hours. But the structure also gives them flexibility to take long periods of time away from work.

It is much easier for newly formed organizations to implement a shared leadership model. More established groups find these transitions difficult. Changing to a team or codirector model can be intimidating to staff and board members, who rely on one person as the final decision maker in the organization. In addition, the model might work for one set of leaders but not for another. Trust, personalities, and structure all play into its success. There might also be a need for codirectors or leadership teams at one time in the organization's stage of development but not in another. As we see in Robby's story, which follows, moving back and forth between a codirector model and a single director can be stressful for the organization, but it can also help with difficult and sometimes untimely situations.

Robby's Story: Directing the SouthWest Organizing Project

The history of the leadership structure at the SouthWest Organizing Project (SWOP) is not unusual for grassroots organizations. Starting as a collective, the organization had its first executive director, Jeanne Gauna, after founder Richard Moore left in 1990 to head up the Southwest Network for Environmental and Economic Justice. Powerful and charismatic leaders, Jeanne and Richard were well known among activists and policymakers throughout the United States. Jeanne often wrote and spoke about the importance of developing new leaders and giving them the opportunities to lead. After turning fifty years old in the mid-1990s, Jeanne was beginning to think about new leadership for SWOP, and as a result she and the board moved to make Michael Leon Guerrero, a younger colleague, her codirector. In addition to implementing the codirector model, Jeanne and Michael were encouraging and supportive of emerging youth organizing and leadership development efforts in the late 1990s, a clear acknowledgment of the impending generational shift. These youth organizing efforts not only worked to bring more young people into the organization and address issues that particularly interested them; they also gave younger staff like me the opportunity and political space to develop our own leadership skills by holding greater responsibility to make decisions and supervise a small team of interns. Michael and Jeanne made room for me and other younger staff to be successful, as well as possibly to fail. The time they spent being hands-on mentors and hands-off supporters was invaluable. In early 2000, Jeanne was diagnosed with breast cancer and took a leave of absence from SWOP. In early 2003, she passed away. Soon after Jeanne's death, Michael informed me that he was planning to leave SWOP and move out of state. We put a proposal together for the board that promoted me to codirector in anticipation of Michael's leaving in the following year. When he left, the board made me the sole executive director. It wasn't easy for any of us: we faced Jeanne's death, another transition, and a board that had been for years working with a strong founder.

Having been at the organization for ten years starting as an intern and now as executive director, I am thinking about the future, my transition, and a group of people who can lead us through the next change. Maybe we will have codirectors again or a management team. It is not my decision to make alone, but an important one for the whole organization. What is clear is that it has taken a host of strategies to address our leadership challenges over the history of the organization. We have attempted to address the crisis of "no room at the top" by expanding formal and informal leadership roles; we have broken free and succumbed to the trap of undoable executive director jobs that are unattractive to younger leaders; we have carved out the political space to make younger leaders in the organization visible; and we are once again contemplating another organizational form. The lesson we have learned is one of experimentation and innovation balanced with addressing the immediate needs of the organization while constantly looking to the future.

Creating Room for More Voices

Newer generations looking for more voice in organizations have led to a revival of interest in models of decision making that include the entire staff and even constituents. When young staffers talk about a consensus-based approach, veterans of political groups that formed in the 1960s and 1970s may adamantly insist that collectives do not work. They have memories of collective decision-making process that led to bitter infighting and informal hierarchies that destroyed groups and wreaked havoc in people's lives.[26] Yet younger leaders have been persistent in their efforts to find ways, especially in smaller social change organizations, to institute decision making done by staff members together.

Andrew Friedman and Oona Chatterjee started the organizing group, We Make the Road by Walking, in 1997 as codirectors. In their early years they moved to a model of structured collective decision making to include the voices of staff members and made the transition from a self-selecting board to a membership-elected board. Then in 2007 they merged with a sister organization, the Latin American Integration Center (LAIC) to form Make the Road New York. Decision making has changed again with the three codirectors, Andrew, Oona, and LAIC's founder Ana Maria Archila. None of these forms are easy or ideal, but they have not deterred the organization from growing and maintaining its excellent reputation.

In addition to collectives, new leaders are continuing to look for significant ways that staff members can be involved in organizations. Young directors are seeking new models that offer them some middle ground, where they can have meaningful participation even without a shared decision-making model.

Creating an Organization of Partners

Not everyone wants more involvement in overall decision making. For some newer leaders, the goal is to reduce time spent discussing decisions and instead distribute leadership throughout the organization, giving staff members more authority and responsibility for running their own programs. Following a model of pushing down leadership and responsibility, executives in these groups encourage other directors in the organization to develop and fund their own programs, and they are accountable for getting results. The job of the top leader is to bring together the different directors to discuss common issues, make decisions about the overall organization, and call on each other for advice.

In one case, the model works almost like a partnership. New ideas are presented to the leadership group, and they decide whether a new program should be added to the organization based on the value it adds to the mission and whether it can fund itself. The executive director is responsible for raising the money for infrastructure costs, such as incubating new groups not ready to fully stand on their own and seizing opportunities that can be brought to the directors. He sees his role as supporting innovation: pushing the directors to take risks such as including new programs that serve the most marginalized or ignored populations. The leader is well known by funders, and many of the program heads are recognized in their individual fields.

In both this organization and others with a similar model, the executive directors make themselves available as coaches to internal leaders on issues such as working with staff, raising money, and evaluating their work.

What's in the Form?

The four approaches we have described—social entrepreneurship, coleadership, participatory organizations, and partnerships—are examples of how retaining new leadership in the social sector can transform how organizations are run. One new executive director said that he was bringing his large agency into alignment after years of expansion based on funding opportunities rather than on the needs and desires of the community. As he worked through each department, he wondered if there were innovative leadership models that were less hierarchical and achieved results. Next generation and older leaders who are taking over organizations with larger budgets have used nonprofit arms of for-profit consulting firms to help them reorganize the structure and plan for the future. All of these new leaders are determined to make operations work more effectively to serve their communities better.

Not every new model is a success. Some directors pushed power down to create flattened hierarchies, only to find that staffers needed more support and direction. Others discover that decision making stalls when they introduce more participatory approaches. And one group, after a successful period with two young codirectors, floundered when both left. Still the amount of innovation is impressive and hopeful.

As one young leader noted, "No matter what process you set up, it doesn't work unless the executive director has the buy-in and is going to allow that process to affect his or her decision making. . . . Regardless of what format, for us it's been about communications both before and after the decision. . . . If people understand why a decision is made, that's as important as the process."

Gen Xers and millennials are looking to lead in new ways, but they cannot do it alone. They need the help and support of older generations. The final chapter turns to the work the generations need to do together and how their partnership will take us into the future.

Notes

1. Chaudhry, L. "Will the Real Generation Obama Please Stand Up?" *The Nation*, 2007, *285*(18), 11.
2. Carucci, R. A. *Leadership Divided: What Emerging Leaders Need and What You Might Be Missing.* San Francisco: Jossey-Bass, 2006.
3. Siegel, D. *Sisterhood Interrupted: From Radical Women to Grrls Gone Wild.* New York: Palgrave Macmillan, 2007.
4. Cornelius, M., Corvington, P., and Ruesga, A. *Ready to Lead? Next Generation Leaders Speak Out.* Washington, D.C.: The Meyer Foundation, 2008.
5. INCITE! Women of Color Against Violence (ed.). *The Revolution Will Not Be Funded: Beyond the Non-Profit*

Industrial Complex. Cambridge, Mass.: South End Press, 2007.

6. Martin, C. "Generation Overwhelmed." *The American Prospect,* www.prospect.org/cs/articles?article=generation_overwhelmed, October 22, 2007.

7. Solomon, J., and Sandahl, Y. *Stepping Up or Stepping Out: A Report on the Readiness of Next Generation Nonprofit Leaders.* Washington, D.C.: Young Nonprofit Professionals Network, 2007.

8. For more information, see Wells, S., *Changing Course: Windcall and the Art of Renewal.* Berkeley, Calif.: Heyday Books, 2007.

9. Horwitz, C., and Maceo Vega-Frey, J. *Spiritual Activism and Liberation Spirituality: Pathways to Collective Liberation.* May 2006. www.stonecircles.org/thoughts/writing/liberation.html.

10. Draut, T. *Strapped: Why America's 20- and 30-Somethings Can't Get Ahead.* New York: Anchor Books, 2005; Brook, D. *The Trap: Selling Out to Stay Afloat in Winner-Take-All America.* New York: Times Books, 2007.

11. Warren, E., and Tyagi, A. W. "What's Hurting the Middle Class." *Boston Review,* Sept./Oct. 2005.

12. Schwinn, E., and Wilhelm, I. "Nonprofit CEO's See Salaries Rise." *The Chronicle of Philanthropy,* October 2, 2003.

13. For example, Tides Center claims that "[s]ince 1996, Tides Center has been fiscal sponsor to 677 projects with combined revenues of $522.4 million, and has worked with well over 800 projects since the first days as the Projects Program. Tides Center currently manages almost 200 projects." Tides also runs Tides Shared Space, "in response to the ongoing difficulties that social change organizations and nonprofits have in finding quality, affordable work and program space. Workspace is often the second largest budget item after salaries." See www.tidescenter.org.

14. Thanks to Alvin Starks for this insight.

15. Working Group on Nonprofit Careers; Cornelius, M., Corvington, P., and Ruesga, A. *Ready to Lead? Next Generation Leaders Speak Out*. Washington, D.C.: The Meyer Foundation, 2008.

16. Davis, E. "Young Nonprofit Professionals: Preparing the Path for Leadership." October 2007, www.edaconsulting. org; Cornelius, Corvington, and Ruesga. *Ready to Lead?* Interestingly, only one-third of these leaders thought education helped advance them into leadership.

17. Leadership Learning Community, www.leadershiplearning. org.

18. Charan, R., Drotter, S., and Noel, J. *The Leadership Pipeline: How to Build the Leadership-Powered Company*. San Francisco: Jossey-Bass, 2001.

19. Davis, E. "Young Nonprofit Professionals."

20. As described in Blake-Beard, S., Murrell, A., and Thomas, D. "Unfinished Business: The Impact of Race on Understanding the Mentoring Relationship." *Harvard Business School Working Paper*, 2006.

21. Hill, L. A., and Kamprath, N. *Beyond the Myth of the Perfect Mentor: Building a Network of Developmental Relationships*. Cambridge, Mass. Harvard Business Publishing, 1998.

22. Thanks to Patrick Corvington for this insight on how different generations approach shared leadership.

23. Wade, L. C. "Settlement Houses." *The Electronic Encyclopedia of Chicago*, Chicago Historical Society, 2005. www.encyclopedia.chicagohistory.org/pages/1135.html (June 3, 2008).

24. The most often cited critique of collection models comes from Jo Freeman's work. See Freeman, J. "The Tyranny of Structurelessness." In Koedt, A., Levine, E., and Rapone, A., (eds.), *Radical Feminism*. New York: Quadrangle Books, 1973.

25. Field, A. "When the Boomers Leave, Will Your Company Have the Leaders It Needs?" *Harvard Management Update*. Cambridge, Mass.: Harvard Business School

Publishing, 2007; McCormack, K. "Careers: The Goods on Generation Y." *BusinessWeek*, June 2007; Coopersmith, A. "Baby Boomers and Generation X: Generational Values Transforming the Workplace." *San Jose Mercury* and *SiliconValley.com*, January 2000.

26. Freeman, J. "The Tyranny of Structurelessness." *JoFreeman. com*. www.jofreeman.com/joreen/tyranny.htm.

6

LEADING ACROSS GENERATIONS

> I've learned that when we talk story, we should not
> do it in a way that implies that we did it better or
> that we were that great. And we talk as much about
> the mistakes we made, about the regrets we have, as
> we do the successes.
>
> *Baby boomer*

In this final chapter, we look at how understanding the leadership tasks of different generations and the values we hold in common can help lead us through the leadership transitions of the next decades. We also recommend how to start to address systemic issues that ultimately will be resolved through the creative ideas and lived experiences of all generations.

Roles of Each Generation

In Chapter Three we presented the tasks that each generation of social sector leaders performs given their cohort and position in their life cycle, and the ways each of the four generations examined in this book can offer support and integration of other age cohorts or discourage intergenerational work. We have summarized these in Tables 6.1 and 6.2.

Tables 6.1 and 6.2 explain how leadership is a relationship between what you need to accomplish for yourself and what you can do for others. Exercise 6.1, "Reflections on My Roles and Supports," on page 151 is designed to help people explore whether

Table 6.1. Summary: The Generational Leadership Tasks

Millennials: **Development**	• Focus on acquiring skills, information, and experience. • Generate ideas of different approaches to the work and possible roles. • Develop critical analysis of social sector work. • Try different identities.
Generation X: **Establishment**	• Gain mastery and field perspective. • Expand assumptions. • Implement ideas, and deepen work. • Continue to learn, and start directing others. • Solidify relationships.
Baby Boomers: **Assessment**	• Use influence and experience, and unite with others to make change. • Reflect on learning, and teach others. • Promote and support promising leaders to increase their power. • Begin to think of your legacy.
Veterans of Change: **Contribution**	• Have a concrete plan to leave the position, and release power and control. • Support new leaders by using contacts and relationships and sharing ideas and experience. • Reflect on success and analyze failures. • Create role to make a contribution.

Table 6.2. Generational Leadership: Moving Ahead or Staying Behind

What **Veterans of Change Need to Do**	**Mentor and Remind** • Mentor Generation Xers and millennials by listening to their grievances and supporting their desire to make change. • Remind baby boomers that though they are now in power, they should start to prepare the next generation of leadership. • Offer honest assessments of the recent history, and remind others of values and elements of social change. • Listen and reminisce when asked.

What Veterans of Change Should Avoid	**Remain Stuck in Dated Experiences** • Dismiss younger generations, and become disaffected. • Neglect to pass on important information. • Become irrelevant by not keeping up with the interests and needs of younger generations. • Opt out.
What Baby Boomers Need to Do	**Partner and Challenge** • Partner with Generation X in bringing this cohort into leadership, including giving them significant responsibility and authority. • Challenge and push Gen Xers to build leadership skills. • Encourage millennials, giving them acknowledgment and attention. • Acknowledge the work of the veterans of change generation and assure them their legacy will be carried on. • Recognize that social change does not start and end with their generation.
What Baby Boomers Should Avoid	**Resist the Transition** • Refuse to plan for leadership. • Neglect to plan transition in a concrete specific way. • Do not share what and what could differently. • Be unwilling to of decision-making, and organizational may invite younger staff.
What Generation X Needs to Do	**Support and Push** • Support the development of millennials, and learn from their ideas. • Expect pressure from millennials to institute new ways of doing the work. • Push up against baby boomers with both content knowledge and experience from a decade in the field. • Partner with baby boomers to move work ahead and make needed change. • Bridge the millennial and boomer generations. • Learn from veterans of change.

(continued)

Table 6.2.   Generational Leadership: Moving Ahead or Staying Behind (*continued*)

What Generation X Should Avoid	**Defines Leadership in Reaction to Previous Generations** • Remain alienated from other generations, and opt out of leadership. Feel threatened by the millennial generation's passion and confidence. • Become cynical about making an impact, withhold knowledge, and forsake the role of bridging generation gaps. • Look only at what individuals, not systems change, can do.
What Generation X Needs to Do	**Learn and Confront** • Learn from Gen Xers and baby boomers both the content of the work and the way it is currently done. • Raise new ways to do the work. • Make mistakes, and learn from experience. • Respect contributions of older generations, especially boomers and veterans of change. • Connect with and push against Generation X.
What Millennials Should Avoid	**Dilutes Impact and Progress** • Ignore previous generations, and lose ground by not learning from the past. • Move on instincts and passions but without connecting to others. • Ignore analysis of structures and systems that create problems that need to be addressed.

these roles resonate with their own experiences and encourage them to add their own. It is more individually oriented, though it can be done in a group. The exercise helps participants to reflect on their leadership by placing themselves on the charts presented in Tables 6.1 and 6.2. Exercise 6.2, "What Does Each Generation Need to Accomplish," on pages 152–153 is primarily a group exercise to be used with those who are not familiar with the descriptions of roles in this book. It is designed to start a conversation about how different generations of leaders approach their work and ways they can support one another. This exercise can also be used with staff and board members.

Tables 6.1 and 6.2 emphasize the importance of the leader's position in the life cycle and the impact that has on how that person sees and enacts his or her role. It does not indicate what the person will accomplish in terms of the substance of his or her work. Once each generation has a sense of the leadership tasks given to its generation, it is easier to discuss how to support the development of other cohorts in ways that are appropriate for them. Of course, leadership roles are not just about the process; they are also about the content. And that takes us back to our discussion of values and trust.

Exercise 6.1
Reflections on My Roles and Supports

Tables 6.1 and 6.2 present roles each generation can play and how the generations can support one another. Here are some questions to help you reflect on your roles and supports:

- Where am I on each chart?
- In what ways am I accomplishing the tasks of my generation (Table 6.1)?
- In what ways am I supporting other generations (Table 6.2)?
- What could I be doing differently?

Large Group Activity Option

This activity can be adapted for a large intergenerational group. Divide the group into generational cohorts to answer the questions above. This should take about twenty minutes. Have each generation report back to the larger group, and then ask the participants:

- What was particularly helpful about doing this exercise?
- What have you learned about the other generations?

Exercise 6.2
What Does Each Generation Need to Accomplish?

This group exercise can get people to think about the roles of each generation. The participants should *not* be familiar with the information in Table 6.1. This exercise can be done in a variety of settings, such as with the staff and board of an organization at a retreat or in a workshop setting for nonprofit leaders. You can also download this exercise from our Web site at www .workingacrossgenerations.org.

Step 1

Distribute copies of the blank chart at the end of the exercise, allowing lots of space in each column. Ask participants to list the tasks that each generation needs to accomplish. Have participants work alone for five minutes. As an example, the facilitator may want to offer one or two tasks under each generation from the full chart in Chapter Three. But do not show the chart until the end of the exercise.

Step 2

Once everyone in the group has filled out the chart, ask people to share what they have written. Have separate flip chart sheets to record the tasks of each generation. *Important*: Use different color markers, sticky notes, or separate sheets of flip chart paper to distinguish responses by the respondent's generational cohort. For example, use a black marker for comments by Gen X, a blue marker for comments by baby boomers, and so on.

Step 3

After reviewing the responses, ask the group:

- Where do people agree on generational tasks? Where do people disagree? Are there differences in how the chart was filled out by different generations?

Step 4

Ask the group to decide what should be the central role of each generation by posing the question, "What are the most important tasks for each generation?" This exercise will generate a lot of conversation about how we see each other. For example, some people might say there are no differences; others might have conflicts about roles and stage of development. It is important not to get stuck on the details but to stick with the life cycle approach.

Optional

At this point, you can distribute a copy of Table 3.1. You may or may not agree with what we presented in there. We welcome your ideas and suggestions at www.workingacrossgenerations.org.

Step 6

Ask the group how this exercise makes them think differently about the roles they currently play in their organization. If there is time, this can be done through an individual writing activity. Ask for volunteers to share their reflections.

Millennials	Generation X	Baby Boomers	Veterans of Change
Define major role	Define major role	Define major role	Define major role
Specific tasks	Specific tasks	Specific tasks	Specific tasks
•	•	•	•
•	•	•	•
•	•	•	•

Values and Trust

We discussed in Chapter Three how essential it is to understand common values across generations. Values are the underpinning of our work in the nonprofit sector and are essential for social change. Here is a recap of the three components in the values frame:

- *Vision* is the spirit of the organization and describes the world we want to create, not the problems we are trying to solve. The vision keeps everyone moving in the same direction even when tactics or strategies differ.

- *Trust* can come out of a shared vision, or it can create the conditions across generations for building a vision together. Trust is about relationships and implies a shared history or understanding.

- *Awareness*, or consciousness, is a process of learning about the forces that keep the vision from being realized. Awareness guides the activities of an organization through analyses of barriers and opportunities.

These three are mutually reinforcing. Reaching a shared vision may be the ultimate goal, but believing in the vision is based on an analysis of what to do and trust in one another. Trust is one of the largest stumbling blocks between generations. There are many trust-building exercises to help staff members work together, and we think these are useful in intergenerational groups.[1] Another way to start a conversation about trust is to look at the issue of awareness or consciousness.

Intergenerational discussions about consciousness can be difficult when the older generations have an analysis of how systems operate and what leads to change that is not always understood or shared by newer leaders. Long-held views by boomers and veterans of change can offer newer generations important information. And fresh ideas from Generation Xers and millennials can spur activity in areas that have seen little progress over the past several decades. Exercise 6.3 is one way to share different ways of looking at how to make change.

Exercise 6.3
Political Awareness Across Generations

This exercise gives people who work in a multigenerational setting an opportunity to discuss where they learned their analysis of how the world operates and the ways to make change. The goal of this exercise is not to build consensus but to give people a better understanding of each other's political awareness context through listening and sharing.

Step 1

Divide into small, cross-generational groups of four to five people. Show the questions below to everyone (either as a handout or written out on flip chart paper), and tell them that each person in the group will share his or her story based on these questions. Give them about five minutes to prepare their stories.

Questions

The following questions may help you describe your sense of political awareness (conscious/analysis) of how the system of inequality and inequity operates in our society.

- Did you have an "Aha!" moment when this became clear, or did you gradually learn or become aware of the way inequities work in our society?

- Was there someone who particularly influenced your analysis: a family member, a teacher or mentor, a peer?

- Did you learn this through personal or community experience? Was it a result of something you read?

- Did your workplace have a role?

- How old were you when you had this understanding?

(continued)

Exercise 6.3
Political Awareness Across
Generations (*continued*)

- Has your analysis changed over time?

- What did you learn from your elders? What did you learn from those who are younger?

- What helped you with your analysis and awareness? Are there things that got in the way?

Step 2

Ask someone from each group to start the storytelling. Everyone else is asked to listen without interruption until that person is done. A timekeeper should make sure everyone has a turn and that there is enough time left over for a discussion in the small group about similarities and differences that participants heard. We recommend that each person is given four to five minutes for storytelling and about fifteen to twenty minutes for a small group discussion.

Step 3

Bring the groups back into a large group, and discuss some of the key similarities and differences identified between generations. What new insights have people learned about their generation and the other generations?

Raising awareness or consciousness is a process that takes place on the job for many nonprofit social change staffers, especially for younger generations who have few venues outside of work for this type of education. Developing methods to help expedite raising awareness, both within and outside organizations, can help all generations not to lose ground in the effort to create a just, equal, and sustainable future.[2] It also helps to build trust.

When we talk about trust between generations, it is important to identify what different generations need. For example, for veterans of change, trust can be about the younger generations' ability to carry on their legacy. Boomers might be looking for new generations to affirm their leadership and hard work. Trust for Gen Xers could be the opportunity to do the work differently. Millennials' view of trust is still forming and might have more to do with trying to use new tools to make a larger impact. Trust requires reassurance and letting go.

Robby's story about trust is an example of how trust can be assumed, contested, and then built.

Robby: Building Trust and Sharing a Vision

There we were, three generations of social justice activists, in the SouthWest Organizing Project (SWOP) basement, staff and board members, sitting around the table talking about strategy. Before long we were disagreeing. SWOP had a long and successful history of organizing and direct action. But from the staffers' point of view, this was not enough. SWOP members continued to pack the meetings at city hall to advocate for our issues. Yet we would be outvoted by the city council 8–1 or 7–2. It seemed clear to staff that we needed to adopt electoral strategies, including encouraging SWOP members to run for the council, targeting get-out-the-vote efforts, and building power to hold officials accountable. But the older board members were balking at the idea. They wanted to remain a smaller watchdog organization with fiercely independent politics. Our role was to push from the outside, they said, not to get involved with large voter mobilizations.

We had backed into a discussion about the type of change we felt the organization was capable of achieving, and I found myself wondering if there was more to what people were saying than what was in their words.

I had learned quickly after becoming executive director that the trust and confidence my mentors had in me to lead the organization did not necessarily extend to the board of directors and other long-time members. While the board respected me and felt I had the potential to lead and manage, we had no history together at that level. After Jeanne Gauna, SWOP's founder, died and Michael, a long-time staffer and briefly my codirector, left the organization, the board started to look over my shoulder. My minor decisions were scrutinized; board members would bypass me in talking with staff members.

For example, the board chair wanted to know how I was supervising staff. I showed her our work plan, including each staff member's objectives and evaluation measures. She felt reassured, but I was upset that I had to provide her with such detailed evidence of my competence. The board treasurer kept questioning my expenditures, but when we went through our first year and the organization was in the black, he eased up. Yet I began to take their questions and criticisms personally, adding a layer of suspicion and creating a vicious cycle of mistrust between us.

Later these board members talked about the trauma and responsibility they felt when they lost Jeanne and then Michael. They were unsure of their role and did not want the organization to fall apart. And they didn't really know me the way they had known Jeanne and Michael. So why should they just sit back and assume I would know what to do?

Back at our meeting in the SWOP basement, I felt I was carrying on Jeanne's legacy, since she had discussed this change with me before she passed away. It didn't occur to me that the board members, who had known Jeanne much longer than I had, also thought they were preserving her legacy. The board chair wanted to include

our membership more in decision making, so we worked
hard to return to regular and well-attended membership
meetings. The treasurer feared that all his work in keeping
the organization ahead financially would be undone by
unchecked spending in a new area. We had to prove that
the funding was there to support a more ambitious vision.

Fortunately, there was the bridge builder, Joaquin, a
boomer staff member who had similar political experiences
to the older board members and was also active in the
staff meetings. He was unsure if an electoral strategy
was the right way to go, but he also thought that the old
assumptions that change would be made by staying outside
the political system had not worked. He decided greater
electoral involvement was worth trying, and talking with
residents about elections would, at the very least, help
continue to build SWOP's membership base. Joaquin
played the bridge builder role by letting older SWOP
members and board members express their fears. He took
a risk by placing his trust in me.

In the end, long-time board members were more open
and supportive of new approaches to the work once we
reaffirmed our commitment to grassroots organizing and
to being a membership organization, including member
involvement in organizational decision making.

When I think back to that meeting in the basement,
I realize there were ways I could have eased the tension
earlier. It would have been good to have had one-
on-one conversations with board members and asked,
"What's important to you?" or "What was it about your
relationship with Jeanne and Michael that led you to trust
them?" or "What are your fears?"

It took a lot of patience to rebuild trust throughout the
organization. One thing that helped was receiving support

> *from long-time funders to build our capacity and provide me with executive coaching. Perhaps most important, we were all passionate and stubborn because we cared about the organization. That love of SWOP held us together so we could build the trust we needed to move our shared vision forward.*

Trust is often discussed as something that is earned, but it doesn't have to be that way. In his book on generational differences focused on the corporate sector, Carucci offers the radical suggestion that people in the workplace, especially older leaders, extend trust before it is earned.[3] We agree that this would be a better place to start. Trust is a gift that can be offered by older leaders, a hand held out to new generations, and taken away only for cause. This approach both models our values and can push us forward in working together to solve problems. But it will work only if the generations can communicate and discuss their differences.

Conversations: Talk Is Cheap and Necessary

Not everyone believes that the generation gap is a stumbling block in social sector work.[4] The best way to find out is to listen to each other. Learning to talk frankly across generations can be challenging; it both takes and builds trust. It takes trust in the form of patient, real listening, and a willingness to stay engaged with one another to find common ground. Without these dialogues some organizations will find it more difficult to achieve their mission; with them there is a basis for strengthening organizations and the field in order to make effective and lasting change.

We offer some suggestions on how to start these conversations, beginning with how older generations can talk to younger ones and then how younger generations can talk to their elders.

How Older Generations Can Talk with the Younger Generation

We found that baby boom leaders want to know more about the younger generation's worldview and vision for the future. At the same time, they believe that the younger generation needs to learn what has come before them to have a better understanding of current conditions. Yet boomer leaders have mixed results in trying to prepare the next generation for organizational leadership.

Perhaps one reason is that in intergenerational discussions, as in mentoring, the focus is primarily on what older leaders can offer younger leadership and little on what the generations can exchange. In a revealing statement, when asked what older generations could learn from younger ones, a baby boom leader blurted out, "Nothing," then quickly corrected herself. Ultimately both boomers and veterans of change, and Xers and millennials, must be able to approach one another with genuine mutual appreciation and the common goal of making change.

Older leaders frequently dismiss age as a factor in misunderstandings or mistrust when it is raised by Next Geners or they lay the blame on the younger person (calling this person disrespectful or arrogant, for example). Yet when younger leaders feel there is a generational miss, they wonder why boomers and veterans of change do not want to find out why. It can be hard to set aside a negative reaction or defensiveness, but one of the responsibilities of older leadership is to help new leaders. Listening and taking an interest is the first task.

The next task is for boomers and veterans of change to pass on lessons learned to the next generations. Many older leaders understand the importance of transferring information to the younger generations for movement and organization building. They want to talk about their perspectives and decisions in a useful way, not dwelling on the past but engaging in honest storytelling. Here is what one boomer said:

> It's always a challenge talking about the past in a way that's not glorifying the past. It doesn't mean that we did everything right or that we knew exactly what we were doing. It just means that we went through this and we can tell the story and let people judge for themselves . . . [what they] can use. . . . I've tried to do that in a way that's not preaching or paternalistic. I've heard so many people in my generation talk down to the younger people: "Oh, back in the '60s, blah, blah, blah."

They also believe that the next generation can learn from the decisions and strategies of older leaders even if they decide to do things in a new way. And sometimes historical perspective is invaluable in not repeating mistakes:

> They say that this is something new, and we are going to do this. I said no; they promised to do that twenty years ago, and I can tell you the whole history. . . . They have no idea. They thought it was a brand-new concept. [But] it has been around for a long time, but they used to call it this. And I can explain that. It's really important because if they didn't know that particular type of history, they wouldn't know it. And I think that's something we can share.

While some leaders were using staff meetings to create space for intergenerational dialogue, others saw this conversation taking place outside the organization in more informal social settings, perhaps over a cup of coffee or a beer. Few had participated in structured sessions that were devoted to learning across generations.

> ### Talking Across Generations
>
> *Consciously creating a time and place to talk across generations goes a long way in creating understanding between older and younger leaders. Here are some ideas that can help make this type of conversation productive:*
>
> - *Identify and promote existing spaces, activities, and social networks where learning and sharing across generations can be implemented intentionally. Some organizations set aside time during staff-board meetings and retreats and encourage facilitation by an intergenerational team. Several exercises in this book can be adapted to facilitate small or large group intergenerational interactions that can be both fun and thought provoking.*
>
> - *Listen and talk with, not at, each other. Stories and narrative are important ways of sharing information, but they also can cut off interaction. Help younger leaders recognize how they are perceived by boomers and ways they can enter the conversation with a sense of openness.*
>
> - *Develop and provide training on how baby boom leaders can pass on their knowledge and engage with younger leaders.*
>
> - *Pay particular attention to each generation's views on race, gender and gender identity, class, culture, sexual orientation, and other identities.*
>
> - *Bring baby boom and younger leaders together to envision the future of social change and movement building and to think creatively about building organizations and networks to support movement building.*

How Younger Generations Can Talk with the Older Generation

Earlier in the book, we discussed in some detail the issues newer generations face when talking with older leaders. Younger leaders wanted to find out why things evolved in certain ways and were interested in how certain strategies and tactics were chosen and whether they hold up today.

The SWOP story identifies several variables that created distrust between the board and staff members. But for Robby, as a younger leader, generational differences were key. In this case, understanding the external political context was also important. Older leaders had one set of assumptions, younger leaders another. Both sides wanted to be acknowledged, and both brought crucial information to the table. It was also important to be able to express their disagreements without it being seen as a personal attack—either on Robby's competency as a leader or the board's hard work in making change.

Exercise 6.4 is a reflection exercise for different generations. It looks at what younger leaders think of the older generation and how their attitudes influence the way they interact. And it can do the same when older leaders reflect on what they think and do in relation to their younger colleagues. Developing awareness of this link is a positive step in building a more constructive relationship between the generations.

Exercise 6.4
What I Think, What I Do

Complete the table by answering the questions in the top row. If you are an older leader, think about the younger generation. Younger leaders should think about boomer and other older leaders.

Be specific in your answers. Review your responses and answer the debriefing questions following the table.

What Do I Think or Say About Baby Boom/Generation X/Millennial Leaders (Including Staff, Board, Colleagues)?	How Does This Influence How I Communicate/Work with the Baby Boom/X/Millennial Generation?	How Do They Respond to Me When I Communicate/Work with Them?
•	•	•
•	•	•
•	•	•
•	•	•

(continued)

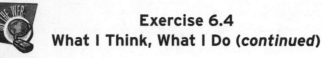

Exercise 6.4
What I Think, What I Do (*continued*)

Debriefing Questions

- What steps can I take to move toward a positive and constructive relationship with the other generations in my organization and field?

- What prevents me from taking these steps?

- Who could help me move forward to treat the other generations' leadership with generosity and respect?

Using the Bridgers

In Robby's story about SWOP, Joaquin played a vital role: he was a bridger. There are bridge builders in all generations. And there is also a generation that often sees itself as bridgers, as described next. Identifying facilitators or bridge builders to improve communications between older and younger leaders can help promote trust and learning across generations.

> ### The Bridge Generation
>
> *Nicole is in her mid-forties. She has close friends and mentors who are boomers ranging from age fifty to sixty. But she is equally at home with her friends and mentors who are in their early to mid-thirties. She identifies with many of the cultural benchmarks of the baby boomers, although she was too young to have participated in the anti–Vietnam War marches and the women's movement. Nicole can also identify with many of the cultural icons of Generation X but often feels "older" than her friends and is not as knowledgeable about their cultural reference*

points. Ronald Reagan was president when Nicole was in college, and she remembers the country's shift to the political right during that time. Few of her peers were interested in working for social change after graduation, and Nicole does not see many social change activists of her age group around her. Some authors have referred to Nicole's in-between age cohort as "shadow boomers" or "cuspers."[5] In fact, Nicole often feels she plays the role of the bridge between the baby boom generation and Generation X. She finds that she brings friends and colleagues of both generations together in social and work settings. At other times, she helps to smooth out potential tensions between her friends when one generation seems to dismiss the other's experience. She listens and then offers constructive feedback on how such comments may sound to the other generation. Nicole feels her role in helping people to cross the generation divide is part of building a strong movement for change.

Recommendations for Moving Forward

Generational shift in leadership is not simply about individuals; it is also about the context in which social sector work takes place. Boomers' fears about their ability to retire or younger generations' worries about how to work and spend time with family are not just personal problems to solve, but larger issues that need to be addressed. The exercises throughout this book can help form a basis for making a difference. But working for social change has schooled us in how individuals alone cannot solve systemic problems.

We end this chapter and the book with recommendations for actions in four areas that are needed to address structural and personal barriers facing social change leaders in both generations: balance between work life and personal life, new ways of leading, financial literacy, and developing trust between generations.

Balancing Work Life and Personal Life

The theme of balance is hard to ignore when thinking about issues facing new generations of leaders. Although younger leaders most often raised this issue, boomers are thinking of balance as well as they contemplate how they can stay involved but work fewer hours. Some of the places to start include these:

- *Make the job doable (and get it done).* There needs to be a sustained effort to start thinking seriously about the structure, culture, and funding streams of small and midsized social sector organizations that require tremendous sacrifice from those in executive positions. Mission-driven work is not the same as for-profit business, but a level of sacrifice over time can make productive and effective change less likely. Leaders are now rewarded for putting in long hours and taking heroic measures for their organizations. This places an undue burden on the director, creates impossible expectations for the next leader, and diminishes credibility for the sector at large.

- *Support new norms for executive jobs.* Leaders and board members should work together on sectorwide solutions for how to create reasonable standards for the job. Expectations of social sector directors are in part created by a generation of leaders who were able and willing to dedicate exceptional amounts of time to their work. But boards of directors and funders also have a role in reevaluating the assumptions of what it takes to lead and fund organizations to do their work.

- *Create different funding expectations.* Funders, including government, foundations, corporations, and private donors, all want to get the most for their "investment" in social sector organizations. But there is a pending crisis among nonprofit directors and staffers who are expected to operate their organizations on shoestring budgets and sacrifice the very benefits they are advocating for their clients and constituents. There needs to be a new partnership among funders, boards, and organizational leaders to recalibrate pay, benefits, and time at work that aligns with the vision organizations are working toward.

- *Move beyond the heroic leadership model.* New leaders should receive training on how to combine sound leadership and management skills. Leaders are often seen as charismatic and managers as mundane workhorses. Although heroism and charisma can be wonderful attributes to create change, most social sector leaders must both lead and manage. The leadership literature stresses that in these changing times, organizations thrive on more distributed leadership and joint decision making.[6]

New Ways of Leading

Both older and younger generations want to have an impact. For boomers and veterans of change, the desire to continue to make a contribution to the field may keep them in their positions. Younger leaders seek ways to transform the leadership roles and the decision-making structures within organizations. This time of transition is ripe for challenging current assumptions about leadership and organizational form:

- *Use new leadership ideas.* Seek out and codify new ways of leading, such as codirectorships, shared leadership, and multigenerational leadership teams. These can lure young leaders to stay in the field and facilitate older leaders' needs to reduce their workload.
- *Develop participatory structures.* Document ways that staffers can have meaningful participation in the organization. With all the emphasis on democratic practice, many social sector organizations can seem oddly misaligned between their

external goals and their internal practices. No one wants to waylay important work, but paying attention to participation that works is worth time and investment. A well-structured process may give groups an edge in their work.

- **Consider new ways to finance organizations.** There is constant talk in the sector about new capital financing, but little discussion of what this means for leading organizations. A link is needed between the discussion about funding and sustainability of social sector work and the implications for training and supporting new leadership.

- **Combine boomer experience and Gen X savvy.** With the help of those with experience and expertise in organizational culture, structure, behavior, and form, we can work with boomers and Xers to advance a new culture in organizations. Older and younger leaders want to do a good job, run functional organizations, build the field, and have an impact on social change. There is no reason we cannot be more effective, but it will take a new look that goes beyond outcome frames at how organizations can best support these activities in the years to come. This is an important moment for leaders to think beyond their individual organizations to new ideas of what will constitute field and movement building for long-term change. We should rethink assumptions that the current way social sector groups are structured and operate is the best practice. Instead, we need to build on what works at the same time we allow for the invention of structures that will meet future needs.

Financial Literacy

We know that both older and younger leaders are worried about their financial situations. But there is little information about what these different cohorts need to allow them to leave the sector or entice them to stay. If we believe people can live, lead, and retire on nonprofit compensation scales, then there should be figures to back this up and wide-scale financial information for executives, staff, and board members to put their minds at rest as much as possible:

- **Conduct research on finances.** It would be invaluable to learn the real income, benefits, assets, and debt load that nonprofit leaders and staff are carrying. Research on this issue could go a long way to helping to figure out how to set reasonable pay scales and benefits in the sector. Adding information to current compensation surveys and making the results widely available could provide the field with important information on the collective personal financial issues facing leaders and their staffs. The information would also help integrate social sector needs into larger government policies.

- **Develop financial literacy programs.** There should be wide-scale programs available for nonprofit staffers and leadership that offers information on issues such as what people need in order to retire or cut down on their work at the end of their career, what it will take to retire student debt and other loans, and how much money newer generations need to make depending on the region they live in and their household configuration. Right now individuals figure this out on their own and they are left feeling vulnerable and uncertain about their future.

- **Create mechanisms to make benefits more available to social sector leaders and staff.** Nonprofits lose potential leadership when they cannot pay or offer base benefits to keep staffers in the sector. Individual organizations are constantly threatened by rising health care, retirement savings, and other benefit costs. There needs to be more support for infrastructure and membership organizations that are developing ways that small and midsized groups together can achieve economies of scale to address this problem. There could also be more ways to model on successes such as the National Organizers Alliance pension plan or the Freelancers Union that base plans on individuals (portable) rather than organizational affiliation.[7]

- *Integrate financial literacy into the work.* Financially literate staff will be better able to discuss and address the issues in their organizations' policies and programs. These programs can help show the links between how staffers deal with money and the larger issues facing those living in the United Sates, ranging from taxes to remittances for family members out of the country.

Developing Trust Between the Generations

So much of this book has focused on working across generations that we add this last area with the belief that we can move together toward a vision of change:

- *Understand that building trust is a process, not a problem.* When differences arise between generations, there is often a rush to find a quick fix and move on. Building trust is a process, not a problem to be solved. It may take dedicated time to unpack conflicts and to affirm the commonalities.

- *Create an environment for open conversations.* People need to be able to take risks without being met with defensiveness or anger. Organizations, from the board through the constituents, can retool to support open conversations about ideas on leadership and work-related issues.

- *Recognize power.* One of the most difficult parts of intergenerational relationships is recognizing differences in power. Acknowledgment about power differentials based on age and position will help to move groups out of a victim role into one where power and influence can be shared.

- *Check out assumptions.* It's easy for one group, or one person, to believe they know what another group or person is

thinking. We heard a wide range of views among the generations, and we heard lots of assumptions. We recommend that
checking out these views become common practice.

- *Adjust for styles.* Different people and different generations
  communicate in different ways. Think about the ways each
  of you are comfortable getting to know someone else, and
  integrate this understanding into building intergenerational
  relationships.

- *Be generous of spirit.* We are in a time of change, not just in
  generations, but in all aspects of our lives. This creates enormous pressure to act fast, but we also must take the time to be
  open and generous with one another in order to succeed in our
  common vision for social change and greater justice for all.

Up Next

How can we not be hopeful? We have met and worked with so
many people in the social sector across generations who bring
amazing talent, ideas, passion, skills, and commitment to this
work. Generation change is one part of the future that we can
all create together—if we choose to do so.

> ### Robby's Story Continues: An Epilogue and Looking Ahead
>
> *Looking back at the past four years, generational change
> in leadership at SWOP posed challenges and tremendous
> opportunities for all of us. What seemed like a transition
> in one executive director turned out to be the beginning of
> organization-wide changes that were marked by clashes
> of perspectives and feelings, countless hours of difficult
> and courageous conversations, and forging of a new
> organizational culture. At times, our differences seemed to
> reach a breaking point, only to be glued back together by*

our belief that the vision and work of SWOP was important and that we had to work together to accomplish this.

We are not waiting for the next leadership transition to put our lessons into practice. We are sharing our stories with other organizations and funders, and asking for their ongoing support. To make the executive director's job more sustainable, we are creating more leadership opportunities for our staff organizers so that I am no longer the only "face" of SWOP. I am also considering going on a short leave by taking advantage of retreat programs to give me the space to step back and offer others in the organization the opportunity to stretch their leadership while I am gone—a test drive for future leadership transitions.

SWOP now has a more intergenerational board and has committed to ongoing board development work. I remind myself to ask them "what's important to you?" and "what fears do you have?" when we seem to get stuck along generational lines on decisions. We take the time to have one-on-one conversations outside board meetings. We are looking to identify more bridge-builders like Joaquin both within SWOP's and among our trusted allies.

On the one hand, Generation Y is more visible than ever in our organization and in other groups. On the other hand, that is not the whole story. This year, the former board chair, one of SWOP's boomer founders who challenged our new vision, gave us an incredible gift. She decided to run for state representative, using the electoral strategies that she had been so skeptical of in that meeting in the SWOP basement soon after I became the director. Some of us are helping with her campaign and we plan to win.

We all have changed, and we will keep moving forward—together.

Generation Y is more visible than ever in our organization and in other groups. Changes are not always easy, but the growth and learning opportunities they can bring personally, organizationally, and we are on our way to a better world are certainly worth the journey.

Notes

1. For more on the transformation that takes place for staff members in social change organizations, see Chetkovich, C., and Kunreuther, F., *From the Ground Up: Grassroots Organizations Making Social Change*. Ithaca: Cornell University Press, 2006.
2. For example see, "Project South Building a Movement Institute and Popular Education Program," www.project-south.org/pages/BAM_pages/BAM_intro.htm.
3. Carucci, R. *Leadership Divided: What Emerging Leaders Need and What You Might Be Missing*. San Francisco: Jossey-Bass, 2006.
4. Deal, J. *Retiring the Generation Gap: How Employees Young and Old Can Find Common Ground*. San Francisco: Jossey-Bass, 2006.
5. Gillon, S. *Boomer Nation: The Largest and Richest Generation Ever and How It Changed America*. New York: Free Press, 2004; Lancaster, L. C., and Stillman, D. *When Generations Collide: Who They Are. Why They Clash. How to Solve the Generational Puzzle at Work*. New York: HarperCollins, 2002.
6. For example, Fletcher, J. *The Paradox of Post Heroic Leadership: Gender Matters*. Boston: Center for Gender in Organizations, Working Paper, No. 17, 2003; Hock, D. "The Art of Chaordic Leadership," *Leader to Leader 15* (Winter), 2000; Senge, P. "Leadership in Living Organizations." In Hesselbein, F., Goldsmith, M., and Somerville, I. (eds.), *Organizations Without Walls* (Ch. 7, pp. 73–90). San Francisco: Jossey-Bass, 2001.
7. National Organizers Alliance Web site, http://noacentral.org/page.php?id=5 (May 23, 2008); Freelancers Union Web site, www.freelancersunion.org/insurance/index.html (May 12, 2006).

Selected Resources

Research and Reports

Annie E. Casey Foundation, Executive Transition Monographs Series, www.aecf.org/home/knowledgecenter/publicationsseries/ executivetransitionmonographs.aspx.

Building Movement Project

> *Up Next: Generation Change and the Leadership of Nonprofit Organizations* (Frances Kunreuther, 2005), www.buildingmovement .org/artman/uploads/up_next_001.pdf.

> *Next Shift: Beyond the Nonprofit Leadership Crisis* (Frances Kunreuther and Patrick Corvington, 2007).

> *What's Next: Baby Boom–Age Leaders in Social Change Nonprofits* (Helen S. Kim and Frances Kunreuther, 2007), www.building movement.org/artman/uploads/what_s_next.pdf.

Commongood Careers, *The Voice of Nonprofit Talent in 2008* (2008), www.cgcareers.org/downloads/CGC_2008TalentSurveyReport.pdf.

CompassPoint, Annie E. Casey Foundation, Meyer Foundation, and Idealist.org, *Ready to Lead? Next Generation Leaders Speak Out* (Marla Cornelius, Patrick Corvington and Albert Ruesga, 2008), www.compasspoint.org/assets/521_readytolead2008.pdf.

GrantCraft, *Executive Transitions: Grant Makers and Nonprofit Leadership Change* (Angela Bonavoglia and Anne Mackinnon, 2006), www.grantcraft.org/pdfs/transitions.pdf.

Grantmakers for Effective Organizations

> *Geo Action Guide: Supporting Next-Generation Leadership* (March 2008), http://geofunders.org/geopublications.aspx.

> *The Departing: Exiting Nonprofit Leaders as Resources for Social Change* (Jan Masaoka, 2007), http://geofunders.org/geopublications.aspx.

Idealist.org, *The Idealist Guide to Nonprofit Careers for Sector Switchers* (Steven Pascal-Joiner, 2008), www.idealist.org/sectorswitcher.

Movement Strategy Center, *ReGeneration: Young People Shaping the Environmental Justice Movement* (Julie Quiroz-Martinez, Diana Pei Wu, and Kristen Zimmerman, 2005), www.movementstrategy.org/media/docs/5548_ReGenReport.pdf.

NP2020 Conference, Aim Alliance, and the Johnson Center, *NP2020: Issues and Answers from the Next Generation* (Maria Gajewski and Susan Morales-Barias, 2007), www.np2020.wikispaces.com/space/showimage/NP2020_Web.pdf.

Young Nonprofit Professionals Network, *Stepping Up or Stepping Out: A Report on the Readiness of Next Generation Nonprofit Leaders* (Josh Solomon and Yarrow Sandahl, October 2007), www.ynpn.org/national/YNPN_SteppingUp.pdf.

Resources for Leadership Transition and Development

Alliance for Nonprofit Management: An association of individuals and organizations devoted to improving the management and governance capacity of nonprofits through conferences, networking, and member benefits. www.allianceonline.org.

Bridgespan Group: An organization working to strengthen the ability of nonprofits by providing strategy consulting, sharing knowledge, and helping them to develop strong leadership teams through the Bridgestar initiative. www.bridgespangroup.org.

CompassPoint: A consulting, research, and training organization that provides nonprofits with tools and strategies to help bring about change in these communities. www.compasspoint.org.

Management Assistance Group: An organization that provides support to nonprofit groups struggling with organizational problems or challenges in change or growth. www.managementassistance.org.

National Community Development Institute: A technical assistance and training organization that works to build capacity in low-income communities and communities of color by assisting small organizations, partnering with foundations, and supporting municipalities engaged in social change. www.ncdinet.org/.

Partnership for Immigrant Leadership and Action: PILA operates in the San Francisco Bay Area, providing training and technical assistance to local organizations and communities in order to support grassroots leadership development and electoral organizing. www.pilaweb.org.

Rockwood Leadership Institute: The program specializes in communicating the best practices and strategies in leadership development to the nonprofit community and training sector leaders across the United States and Canada. www.rockwoodleadership.org.

Social Justice Leadership: An organization bringing about social change through its fellowship opportunities, leadership and management programs for grassroots leaders, and assistance to organizations with implementing effective social justice leadership. www.sojustlead.org.

Support Center for Nonprofit Management: A consulting, transition management, and training organization that provides services designed to increase the effectiveness of the nonprofit sector. www.supportctr.org.

Technical Assistance for Community Services: An organization that builds nonprofit strength by connecting people to nonprofits and nonprofits to each other through the sharing of knowledge, skills, and resources. www.tacs.org.

Resources for Personal Renewal

Alston/Bannerman Fellowship: A program that helps to sustain long-time activists of color by providing resources for organizers to take sabbaticals. www.alstonbannerman.org.

Movement Strategy Center: An organization that works to build the movement for social and racial justice by increasing the capacity of individuals and organizations to be strategic, collaborative, and sustainable. www.movementstrategy.org.

Spirit in Action: An organization serving as a catalyst for a strong, unified social justice movement by supporting, sustaining, and connecting individuals who are passionate about social change through leadership programming, training, and various other projects. www.spiritinaction.net.

Stone Circles: An organization that seeks to join together those who are working toward a new paradigm of social change work in an environment that inspires individuals to try new things and reflect seriously on their efforts. www.stonecircles.org.

Vallecitos Mountain Refuge: A center that seeks to support and empower citizens to be effective change makers and social entrepreneurs through retreat programs and training. www.vallecitos.org.

Windcall Institute: An organization that is dedicated to helping organizers and leaders in the social, economic, and environmental justice movements stay committed to their respective causes by inspiring individuals to rediscover their purpose, continue in their role, launch new efforts, and create sustainable work cultures. www.commoncounsel.org/windcall%20institute.

Resources for Younger or Emerging Leaders

21/64: A nonprofit consulting division of the Andrea and Charles Bronfman Philanthropies, 21/64 offers consultation, resource materials, networks, and communication vehicles to individuals, families, businesses, foundations, and federations in times of generational transition. www.2164.net.

Craigslist Foundation: Nonprofit Bootcamp: A one-day program designed to educate and empower the next generation of nonprofit leaders and social entrepreneurs through workshops, speakers, one-on-one coaching, and professional development. www.craigslistfoundation .org/bootcamp.

Emerging Practitioners in Philanthropy: An organization working to strengthen the next generation of grant makers through leadership programs, networking opportunities, and advocacy resources. www.epip.org.

Nonprofit Workforce Coalition: A network of organizations, foundations, and academic centers that exists to connect talented young people to careers in the nonprofit sector and help organizations recruit and cultivate new leadership. www.humanics.org/coalition.

NP2020: A conference initiative designed to give emerging leaders a voice in the nonprofit sector. http://nonprofit2020.wordpress.com.

Perspectives from the Pipeline: A blog by Rosetta Thurman, an emerging nonprofit leader of color, that shares career advice, management resources, and inspiring ideas on the nonprofit sector. http://fromthepipeline.blogspot.com.

Resource Generation: An initiative that works with financially wealthy young people to help them align their personal values and political vision with their financial resources. www.resourcegeneration.org.

Young Nonprofit Professionals Network: One of the nation's largest associations of nonprofit workers, YNPN works to maintain and strengthen the next generation of nonprofit leaders through professional development, networking, and social opportunities. www.ynpn.org.

Resources for Older Leaders

AARP: The leading nonprofit for Americans age fifty years and older that offers its members information relevant to their age group, an organized body advocating on important issues, and many other services geared to benefiting boomers. www.aarp.org.

Civic Ventures: An organization that seeks to engage baby boomers in solving social problems through service programs, grant distribution, and resource networks. www.civicventures.org.

National Council on Aging: The Council's RespectAbility initiative seeks to help nonprofit organizations make more effective use of older Americans in their community-based efforts. www.ncoa.org/content.cfm?sectionID=213.

The Conference Board: The Research Working Group on Managing an Aging Workforce in the Nonprofit Sector is addressing challenges related to aging and a multigenerational workforce in the social sector. http://www.conference-board.org/workingGroups/wkgGrp-Describe.cfm?Council_ID=246.

About the Authors

Frances Kunreuther directs the Building Movement Project, which works to strengthen U.S. nonprofits as sites of democratic practice and advance ways the nonprofit sector can build movement for progressive social change. She is also a senior fellow at the Research Center for Leadership and Action at New York University. She has written numerous articles on generation change and social change and is coauthor of *From the Ground Up: Grassroots Organizations Making Social Change* (2006).

The Building Movement Project was founded while she was a fellow at Harvard University's Hauser Center for Nonprofit Organizations. During her five years at the center, she worked on the intersection of movement building and nonprofit organizations. She headed the Hetrick-Martin Institute for lesbian and gay youth for seven years and in 1997 was awarded a year-long fellowship from the Annie E. Casey Foundation. During her time at Hetrick-Martin, the organization was selected for the 1993 Outstanding Organization in Public Service award from the American Society for Public Administration, as a model program by the Child Welfare League of America (1993), and for the American Institute of Architects' Award for Excellence.

Kunreuther has worked with immigrants, homeless families and children, domestic violence and sexual assault survivors, runaway and homeless youth, and substance users during her thirty years in the nonprofit sector. She has been the recipient of numerous awards, including the Ms. Foundation's Gloria

Steinem Award (1996) and the 1992 Mayoral Award for Leadership honoring Women's History Month.

Helen Kim is part of the bridge generation between the baby boomers and Generation X. She has eighteen years of experience in working with nonprofit organizations as staff, board member, trainer, and consultant. As an independent consultant to nonprofit organizations, Kim has focused her work on leadership development, organizational development, and executive coaching to grassroots and national organizations and foundations in the United States and Korea.

She is an affiliated consultant with the French American Charitable Trust's Management Assistant Program. Kim has facilitated many local and national strategic conversations on issues that include supporting the next generation of executive directors of color, increasing civic engagement in the nonprofit sector, and social justice movement building strategies.

Prior to her consultant work, Kim worked as a community organizer for Asian Immigrant Women Advocates, where she focused on immigrant and environmental justice issues and coordinated national support for the Garment Workers Justice Campaign from 1992 to 1996.

Since 2001, Kim has been a team member of the Building Movement Project and has worked closely with Frances Kunreuther and Robby Rodriguez on generational change and leadership in the U.S. nonprofit sector. She has also taught at the San Francisco State University Graduate School of Social Work.

Kim emigrated from Korea to the United States when she was twelve years old, and she attended Carleton College and the University of Minnesota Law Center. She is based in Oakland, California.

Robby Rodriguez is the executive director of the SouthWest Organizing Project, a grassroots community organizing group, based in Albuquerque, New Mexico, that was founded in 1980 to realize racial and gender equality and social and economic justice. At the age of twenty-nine, he became the youngest director of SWOP and helped lead the organization through a leadership transition and generational shift.

Since 1997, he has helped to organize New Mexico communities to achieve social change in various capacities with SWOP. Between 1998 and 2001, he was a trainer for the Southwest Network for Environmental and Economic Justice (SNEEJ), the United Methodist Church General Board of Global Ministries, the Lifting New Voices Initiative, and Youth Action. In 1999, he represented SWOP and the SNEEJ at the World Trade Organization meeting in Seattle, Washington. During 2000 and 2001, he was cochair of the Youth Leadership Development campaign of the SNEEJ and a member of the International Environmental Justice Working Group that participated in the World Conference Against Racism. From 2002 to 2005, he was a member of the New Mexico Environment Department's Corrales Air Quality Task Force and the City of Albuquerque/ Bernalillo County Water Resources Advisory Committee. He is a past board member of the New Mexico Non Profit Association and a current board member of the New Mexico Environmental Law Center. Since 2004, he has been a project team member of the Building Movement Project. He has represented the U.S. social justice movement as a speaker, panelist, and trainer throughout the United States and in Mexico, Chile, Paraguay, Switzerland, South Africa, Costa Rica, and Brazil.

He graduated from Cornell University with a degree in sociology.

Index